The

SECRET LANGUAGE

of the

SOUL

The
SECRET LANGUAGE
of the
SOUL

A VISUAL GUIDE TO THE SPIRITUAL WORLD

Jane Hope

CHRONICLE BOOKS
SAN FRANCISCO

The Secret Language of the Soul
Jane Hope
First published in the United States in 1997
by Chronicle Books

Managing Editor: Catherine Bradley
Editor: Slaney Begley
Designer: Sue Bush
Commissioned Artwork: Alison Barrett, Matthew Cooper, Louisa St Pierre
Picture Research: Cecilia Weston-Baker
Indexer: Drusilla Calvert, Macrex Indexing Services

Library of Congress Cataloguing-in-Publication Data

Hope, Jane, 1945—
The secret language of the soul: a visual exploration of the spiritual world/
Jane Hope
p. cm.
Includes index.
ISBN 0-8118-1862-4 (hardcover). ---ISBN 0-8118-1861-6 (pbk.)
1. Religions. I. Title.
BL98.H65 1997   97-2307
200--dc21   CIP

1 3 5 7 9 10 8 6 4 2

Typeset in Caslon and Delphian
Colour reproduction by Colourscan, Singapore
Printed by Imago, Singapore

Distribution in Canada by
Raincoast Books
8680 Cambie Street
Vancouver, B.C. V6P 6M9

Chronicle Books
85 Second Street
San Francisco, CA 94105
Web Site: www. chronbooks.com

Note: The abbreviations CE and BCE are used throughout this book.
CE Common Era (the equivalent of AD)
BCE Before the Common Era (the equivalent of BC)

*M*ay all beings enjoy happiness and the root of happiness,
May they be free from suffering and the root of suffering,
May they not be separated from the great happiness devoid of suffering,
May they dwell in the great equanimity free from passion,
aggression and prejudice.

Traditional Buddhist prayer

CONTENTS

INTRODUCTION   8

SOUL AND COSMOS

The World Soul   14

The Great Mother   16

The World Axis   18

Cycles of Time   20

Sacred Calendars   22

Sacred Skies   24

The World of Illusion   26

Illusion and Ego   28

Pantheons of the Gods   30

Balancing Heaven and Earth   32

Divination   34

Sacred Space   36

Directory:

    Celestial Realms   38

    Gods   40

    Goddesses   42

BODY AND SOUL

The Soul in the Body   46

Chakras and Meridians   48

Male and Female   50

Sexual Energy   52

Pilgrimage   54

Sacred Dance   56

The Act of Prayer   58

The Way of the Warrior   60

Sacrifice   62

Sickness and Healing   64

Fear of Death   66

Confronting Death   68

Survival of the Soul   70

Directory:

    Sex and Gender   72

    Immortality   74

    Forms of the Spirit   76

NATURE AND THE SOUL

The Sacred Earth   80

Spirits of Nature   82

The Living Landscape   84

Fertility   86

Lines of Force   88

Spirit of the Hunters   90

Dreamtime   92

Directory:

  Air   94

  Fire   96

  Earth   98

  Water   100

  Sacred Animals   102

THE SPIRIT WORLD

Soul Realms   108

Spirit Helpers   110

Stealers of the Soul   112

Dreams and Visions   114

Communicating with the Gods   116

Turning-Points of the Year   118

Perilous Journeys   120

Directory:

  Angels   122

  Heaven   124

  Hell   126

SOUL AND TRANSCENDENCE

Faith   130

The Defeat of Suffering   132

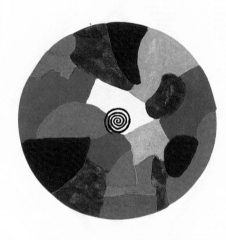

Penitence   134

Vision Quests   136

Toward Non-Attachment   138

Meditation   140

Prayer   142

Retreat   144

Ecstasy and Transformation   146

Teachers of Faith   148

The Path of Ritual   150

The Exceptional Life   152

Paradise   154

Enlightenment   156

Directory:

  Sacred Figures   158

  Miracles   160

  Sacred Texts   162

Belief Systems of the World   164

Glossary   169

Index   170

Acknowledgments   176

INTRODUCTION

Throughout the ages, belief in an inner "soul" or "spirit" has contributed a unique and valuable dimension to human life. The roots of these words connect with the idea of breathing, the ceaseless movement of the wind over the Earth. Like the wind, the soul is invisible – a vital essence that breathes existence into humanity and the natural world. Our awareness of the spiritual is intuitive, achieved through some deep instinct that speaks to us of the interconnectedness of all living things. It is the soul that informs the compassion we feel for other human beings and that suffuses the mundane with a sense of the sacred. It is the soul that translates incident into experience, knowledge into wisdom.

The subject of this book is the language of the soul, which has usually been expressed in enigmatic and symbolic form. It could not have been otherwise, because profound truths accessible through imagination, religion and myth cannot be laid bare by the analytic power of the intellect. Allegory reveals more than analysis, imagery more than literal description. In Tibet the language of the soul was known as "twilight language", an idiom that blurs the clear and distinct realities of the day into the mysteries and darkness of the night. If the symbolism was obscure, that was in part to give protection to those not yet ready to make the spiritual journey.

In ancient and tribal cultures, the soul's special teachings were passed down by word of mouth from one generation to the next. The traditional literature often has many levels of meaning, reflected by complex accretions of commentary. In Europe, alchemy seems to concern the transmutation of base metals into gold; but for the initiate,

"Le Vent dans les Fleurs au clair de lune"

This painting by Marc Chagall (1887–1985) seeks to evoke through images the complex and mysterious yearnings of the spirit. Such emotions, impossible to depict in literal form, express our most profound desires.

alchemy describes the journey of the soul, transmuting the raw material of the psyche into the shining and incorruptible gold of spiritual fulfilment. In the East, Tantra on the surface is concerned with the fierce, dark forms of deities, bloodstained, wearing flayed skins and stamping on corpses; but its inner meaning is the same transmutation of crude emotions into the exhilarating energies of the enlightened mind. Symbols such as these are still meaningful to us in the West today, as we search for ways to feel and comprehend the truths that elude literal description.

In exploring the lexicon of the soul, we inevitably encounter complications when we consider the relationship of the soul to the body. This opposition is most bluntly felt as an absolute dualism, but we are now learning from more holistic concepts, which inform alternative healing, yoga, meditation, and many other manifestations. In the East, the body has never been seen as distinct from the soul. The "psychosomatic" or "subtle" body contains a network of energy channels which move spiritual energy around a complex internal network. More prevalent in Western societies was the view that the body, with its animal instincts and impermanent nature, was inferior to the soul – denial of the pleasures of the flesh allowed the soul to escape contamination and free itself from the shackles of material existence. Similarly, in Buddhist belief, attachment to the world is the source of suffering. In striving toward spiritual self-understanding, we must engage with

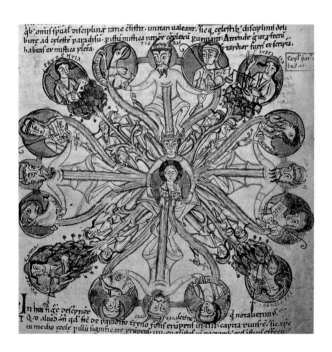

Emblems of Christianity
This figure, from a devotional commentary of the 12th century, depicts the complex network of spiritual symbols underpinning Christian beliefs.

these ideas in a way that makes sense to us. Do our emotions have a spiritual dimension, or can they undermine the spirit? How can we live spiritually with our bodily appetites?

An individual soul or spirit exists in a realm apart, beyond the confines of ordinary time and space. Far from being personal, the soul may participate in the soul of the world itself, the *anima mundi*. Every natural presence in the world – rivers, trees, animals, birds, plants – is perceived to have consciousness, a spiritual essence that living things can share and exchange. When we recognize that the world is "ensouled", our relationship with the environment and all its inhabitants is transformed into respect and appreciation for a shared life. Conversely, when the world is seen as separate from the individual self, feelings of emptiness and disillusion set in – a spiritual listlessness known to tribal peoples as a "loss of soul" and familiar in Western technological societies as *ennui*.

Mustang Effigies
These effigies, hung above the main entrance to a house in Nepal, are intended to ward off evil spirits, believed to be continually present.

Brahma on the Hamsa
*The great Hindu creator god, Brahma, is often depicted on his mount, the wild goose or swan (*hamsa*). The flight of the* hamsa *symbolizes the soul's yearning for release from this life.*

Yet through the various manifestations of faith – vision, symbol, ritual, discipline – we may still grasp the archetypal reality that underlies all experience. Priests and spiritual teachers, acting as intermediaries between human and supernatural realms, have shown us how to achieve inner peace through prayer and meditation – to carve out from the world's incessant din a stillness in which it is possible to hear the needs of the soul. In such sanctified places of heart and mind, we can see the wholeness of being and accept the interdependence of pain and pleasure as the very essence of the human condition.

SOUL AND COSMOS

Our relationship with the Earth and the wider universe is one of humankind's most important spiritual questions. For thousands of years, faiths and belief systems have influenced people's perception of the world around them and informed their awareness and demarcation of time. The oldest religions worshipped the Earth as an all-powerful goddess, the provider of food and shelter who gave birth to all living things and reabsorbed them again after death. Many ancient communities developed sacred seasonal rituals in response to the astronomical movements that they saw in the heavens. Our diverse modern faiths seek to challenge the limitations of a materialistic, secular perspective. They emphasize the soul's place within an orchestrated cosmos, in which spiritual health is essential to personal and universal harmony.

THE WORLD SOUL

In our modern lives, many of us feel disconnected from the natural world. We are no longer dependent upon the pattern of climate and seasons, and have largely abandoned the rituals and sacred ceremonies that once expressed our intimate relationship with the Earth. Yet from the earliest times people have instinctively

sensed a vital, spiritual force linking the whole of the material universe. They believed that the Earth was a living creature, animated by a soul like that of a human being, and this view has been adopted by many ecology movements in the West today. In respecting the sacredness of our Earth, we recognize and acknowledge its connection with the harmony of the individual soul.

This perceived correspondence between the human and natural worlds was once underlined by the elements. The cosmos impacted directly upon early societies in the form of thunder, air, sunshine, stars, mountains, animals and birds. Spirituality was not considered a separate part of existence, and was manifested through veneration for the Earth. Many cultures continue to perceive the sacred in everything around them – all natural phenomena, from stones to mountains, trees to rivers, are thought to possess a soul. The Native American Sioux people believe in *wakan*, a spiritual essence which may exist in both natural and man-made things. Through traditional rituals some societies still attempt to influence the soul of the Earth by prayer, sacrifice and offerings, or by the working of sympathetic magic. Animal masks are often worn in sacred ceremonies – for example, in Africa and Polynesia – to enable the wearer to draw upon the great spiritual power possessed by the animals.

The ancient Greeks' fascination with the world soul was to have a profound influence on Western thought. In

Cosmic Man
During the Middle Ages each zodiac sign was associated with a part of the body, re-affirming correspondences between the individual and an animate universe. A person's physical and spiritual health were believed to be influenced by changes in the stars and planets.

the *Timaeus* Plato used a complex cosmological myth to explain the creation of the universe and the existence of the world soul. The "demiurge", or maker-god, created the universe in the form of a rotating sphere. This sphere, made of soul-matter, was produced by the harmonious fusion of the four elements – earth, water, fire and air. After the creation of the universe, the remnants of soul-stuff were formed into human souls. Translated into Latin, the concept of *anima mundi* re-emerged centuries later to inspire neo-Platonist philosophers, alchemists and astrologers. The spiritual purpose of human beings was thought to lie in rediscovering the universe of ideas – "the fairest and most perfect of intelligible beings" – in which the individual soul originated.

In the 20th century, the psychologist Carl Jung revealed the role that he believed connections between the soul and the cosmos still played in the unconscious. He interpreted spiritual growth as a process that allowed the creative principle animating the universe to become conscious of itself through the human mind – usually through symbols in dreams. Jung's work *Psychology and Alchemy* quotes the alchemist Basilius Valentinus: "The Earth is not a dead body, but is inhabited by a spirit that is its life and soul. All created things, minerals included, draw their strength from the Earth spirit. This spirit is life, it is nourished by the stars, and it gives nourishment to all the living things it shelters in its womb."

Scientific materialism may perceive the world as an inanimate lump of matter, revolving in an essentially empty universe. Yet correspondences between the human soul and the natural world still inform our deeper consciousness through dreams, myths and the symbols of religions that bring spiritual focus to our modern lives.

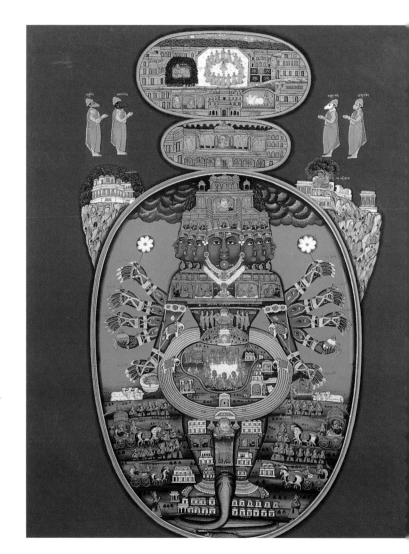

Krishna in Cosmic Form
This Rajasthani painting of 1890 depicts Krishna, the eighth avatar (incarnation) of the Hindu god Vishnu. Krishna's foster mother, Yashoda, once saw the entire universe contained within his mouth. Krishna revealed that he and the world were one and the same.

THE GREAT MOTHER

When we are children, our relationship with our mother is the most important thing we possess. We rely upon her for nourishment and protection, a stronger, powerful being with whom our welfare is inextricably linked. Religions have often venerated the ties between mother and child, and our distant ancestors sensed themselves to be children of a maternal Earth, who nourished and sheltered them. The deepest psychological attachments of individuals are thus interwoven with a community's need to feel close to the patterns of the natural world.

The surface of the Earth itself was thought to be the body of a great and powerful mother, from whose regenerative womb all plant and animal life emerged and into whose arms it was returned in death. The ancient Greeks believed that the folds and undulations of the Earth represented the body of the goddess Gaia. At Delphi the sacred stone called the *omphalos*, or navel (see page 18), formed a spiritual link between Gaia and her progeny – a symbolic umbilical cord which held the spiritual and physical worlds in balance. Violation of the environment is still considered a crime in many beliefs, as shown in this description of a Native American's relationship with the Earth, made less than a hundred years ago: "You ask me to plough the ground? Shall I take a knife and tear my mother's bosom? Then when I die she will not take me to her bosom to rest. You ask me to dig for stone? Shall I dig under her skin for her bones? Then when I die I cannot enter her body to be born again."

At certain sacred locations the landscape was especially revered, particularly where it evoked the female body. Living temples were created from large areas of

The Maternal Goddesses Asherah and Gaia
This detail from the portals of San Zeno Cathedral, Verona, depicts the Canaan Asherah and the Greek Gaia suckling their children.

the natural terrain, such as the massive henge monument at Avebury in southern England. Neolithic peoples worshipped the Earth goddess in great seasonal festivals, linking the human life cycle – birth, puberty, marriage, childbirth and death – to the year's inexorable progress.

The power of maternal Earth goddesses derived from their links with both creative and destructive processes. The ambivalent role of these goddesses – bringers of birth and death, fertility and degeneration – found expression in many cultures as a polarization of imagery. The ancient Indian mother goddess, for example, garlanded with skulls and dripping blood from a long red tongue, survives in the Hindu pantheon as the avenging deities Kali and Durga, while her nurturing qualities

Mother Earth
*In this 11th-century illustration Earth is represented as a woman. Plants growing out of her body, and
the cow and snake suckling at her breasts, emphasize the goddess's role as mother to all living things.*

appear in the gentle Parvati. The Celtic goddess Epona combined the roles of warrior, healer, guardian of the dead and source of fertility, the latter symbolized by the cornucopia with which she is sometimes portrayed.

In Greek myth, the grief of the goddess Demeter brought devastating famine to the world after the abduction of her daughter Persephone by Hades, the god of the underworld. Persephone was subsequently permitted to return to Demeter for half of the year, during which the benign aspects of the goddess flourished. This alternation of the seasons reflects the natural cycle of growth and decay to which all physical life is subject.

The concept of the Earth as a goddess rendered sacred its natural curves and crevices – caves, rock clefts and springs. These were the points at which the body of the goddess opened and through which spiritual connections might be renewed. Several Earth goddesses are linked to the chthonic powers of the underworld, a connection shown by their mastery over snakes and other subterranean creatures. In Attica, initiation rituals into the Eleusinian Mysteries of Demeter enacted a symbolic descent and return of the soul to the underworld.

Aspects of devotion to an Earth goddess still appear in our beliefs today, often in complex, transmuted forms. Many of the environmental concerns of our own time display a re-emerging awareness of our profound connection with the Earth, and of the importance of responsible guardianship for our own spiritual wellbeing.

THE WORLD AXIS

We have always needed to feel ourselves part of a unified, ordered cosmos, whether it is described in scientific or spiritual terms. Aspiring beyond our limited earthly perspective, we imagine distinct but related planes of existence that bring together the gods, our living selves and the souls of the dead. Any sense of isolation from divine powers or revered ancestors has been dispelled in various cultures through the notion of the cosmic axis – a vertical column, like the spinal cord, that joins the separate levels of the universe into a single entity.

This sacred axis provides a central point of time and space, from which all of creation is believed to have arisen. Such a symbolic place, which may be called the Navel of the World, the Sacred Centre, the World Tree or the Cosmic Mountain, frequently represents a point where the gods (or their messengers) revealed themselves to humanity. For example, Mecca, where the Ka'bah, a holy Black Stone, fell from the sky and where God appeared to Ibrahim (Abraham), is the birthplace of the Prophet Muhammad and the central focus for Islamic prayer. Wherever they may be, Muslims at prayer orientate themselves to face the shrine at Mecca.

The Dome of the Rock in Jerusalem is another example of a world axis in an actual geographic location. The present-day Islamic shrine is built on the site of the ancient Jewish Temple of Solomon, described in a rabbinical text as the centre of the world. The foundation stone of the Temple – and of the Jewish world – is set at the heart of the Muslim shrine. Like the sacred, conical rock called the *omphalos*, which formed part of the ancient Greek temple of Apollo at Delphi, this marked the navel of a spiritual universe.

The central axis is often believed to be an aid to visionary experience – a focus enabling the soul to reconnect with a greater reality. Aboriginal peoples in Australia believed that when Numbakula, the divine being, created the ancestors in mythical time, he also made a Sky Pole from the trunk of a gum tree. After consecrating this with his own blood, Numbakula disappeared into the sky. This pole came to represent the centre of the tribe's world. They took the pole with them wherever they travelled, to retain a link with their creator through the cosmic axis. Should the pole break, the clan would face spiritual disorientation, illness or even death.

The World Tree is a universal symbol uniting the spatial realms of experience. Its branches spread out high into the light and the heavens; its trunk is accessible from the surface world; and its root system grows deep into the darkness of the underworld. Gods and human beings maintain their connection with each other through the three diverse realms. In the three-tiered Mayan cosmos, the sacred Ceiba tree enabled the souls of the human dead, as well as the gods, to progress up to heaven. Ascents into the sky are a key feature of

The Centre of the Universe
The sacred axis in the cosmos reinforces the link between human and heavenly realms. This 16th-century Turkish chart, from The Fine Flower of Histories, *shows the Sun at the heart of the universe.*

The Jesse Tree
Divine lineage is sometimes seen as an axis extending through time. The prophet Isaiah perceived a "shoot" growing from the "stump" of Jesse, the father of King David, reflecting their line's link with the future Messiah. This fresco places Christ in the tree's branches.

Yggdrasil, the World Tree
In Norse myth the layers of the cosmos were united by the World Ash, Yggdrasil. The tree's roots extended into the underworld, which included a land of giants and a realm of the dead. The gods were believed to dwell in Asgard, high in the heavens.

shamanism; the journey often involves a symbolic ascent of the World Tree, usually in an ecstatic state, to bring back guidance and predictions from the spirit realm.

To the Native American Navaho, the sacred corn plant represents the world axis, emerging each spring from the darkness of the underworld and growing toward the sky. The successful harvest of corn was essential to survival on the Plains, and the crop played a major role in the ceremonies and rituals of many tribes.

In Tibetan Buddhism a map known as a *mandala* is constructed from coloured sand, showing the symbolic landscape encountered in the journey through meditation to enlightenment. The *mandala* guides the traveller toward the spiritual centre, reached by climbing to the top of the Cosmic Mountain, sometimes known as Mount Meru, where the meditator unites with the deity.

Mount Meru also forms the sacred axis at the heart of the cosmos in both the Hindu and Jain religions. Shaped like an open lotus blossom, the symbol of spiritual growth and rebirth, it extends upward from the depths of the underworld to the gods' dwelling place in the heavens.

CYCLES OF TIME

The passage of time arouses many complex issues in our lives. As we age, we become increasingly aware of our own mortality and the limitations of our physical existence. This personal experience is set against other, conflicting perceptions of time – a modern, secular vision of limitless progress, in which humankind becomes increasingly sophisticated and skilled, and the very different perspectives of most spiritual beliefs. In contemplating timescales far beyond our own lifespan, we often draw upon these beliefs to point up what is significant in the day-to-day pattern of our lives.

Three of the modern world's major religions – Judaism, Islam and Christianity – place emphasis upon a finite, linear vision of time, beginning with the creation and ending in an apocalypse, after which only spiritual

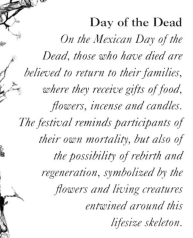

Day of the Dead
On the Mexican Day of the Dead, those who have died are believed to return to their families, where they receive gifts of food, flowers, incense and candles. The festival reminds participants of their own mortality, but also of the possibility of rebirth and regeneration, symbolized by the flowers and living creatures entwined around this lifesize skeleton.

Ra in the Underworld
This image from the Egyptian scribe Userhat's Book of the Dead dates from the 18th dynasty (c. 1400 BCE). It depicts the Sun god Ra making his nightly journey through the underworld in his solar barque before being triumphantly reborn the following morning.

realms will endure. Other belief systems, most notably those of Hinduism, Buddhism and Jainism, draw upon a cyclical view of time in which the cosmos continually renews itself. As the "Wheel of Time" revolves through eternity, worlds are born and die and civilizations appear and disappear; at the completion of each cycle the entire world is destroyed, only to be born again.

In Hinduism the cosmic cycle is interlinked with the concept of *samsara*, in which the individual soul, or *atman*, reincarnates repeatedly. The ultimate spiritual goal is to achieve *moksha*, a state of spiritual perfection that enables the soul to escape from all worldly ties. Hindus believe that, according to the law of karma, the moral implications of our behaviour and actions in each life contribute to the soul's destiny in the next. Virtuous, non-egotistical conduct enables the individual to maintain a spiritual progress through many different lives.

The origin of the cosmic cycle itself is surrounded by many different myths. One tells of the creator god, Brahma, emerging on a lotus from Vishnu's navel and beginning to emit the matter of the universe. The time-scale is immense: one whole day of Brahma's life is equivalent to 8,640 million human years, and Brahma lived for 100 years. Every day of Brahma's life, the god's eyes slowly open and close 1,000 times; each time they open a universe appears and each time they close it vanishes again. Each universe moves through four ages or *yugas*, starting out with the Krita Yuga, the Golden Age, and ending with the Kali Yuga, our own age, in which suffering is all-pervasive.

One of the most celebrated Hindu images is Shiva in the role of Nataraja, Lord of the Dance. The god's cosmic dance represents the continual cycle of destruction and regeneration in the universe, symbolized by the surrounding circle of flames.

The Jains depict the cosmic round as a wheel with six ascending and six descending sections. The spokes represent the ages of the world; the ascending ones move from darkness to light and the descending ones from a noble age into a degenerate one. In the greatest age, shown by the first descending section, people were many miles tall and passed directly into the world of the gods when they died without the need for any religion. In the second realm, human needs were supplied by wish-fulfilling trees – the leaves provided utensils, food and light, and the bark fine clothes. It is said that the Earth was as sweet as sugar and the ocean as delicious as wine. During the descent, sorrow and decay entered the world; in the darkest age at the bottom of the wheel, deadly plagues emerged, the harvests failed and storms and violent tempests shook the Earth. At that point, when all seemed hopeless, the ascent toward the Golden Age began again. Jains believe that the cycle will continue to revolve over the aeons for all eternity.

In ancient Egypt, the actions of the powerful creator god were interwoven with the daily course of the Sun through the heavens. The Sun god Ra, born from the sky goddess at dawn, declined into old age in the evening. Each night the god travelled in a barque across the underworld, where he did battle with the serpent Apep to ensure rebirth the next day. In a universe both perpetually renewed and permanently imperilled, symbols of regeneration, such as the dung-pushing scarab beetle, assumed talismanic importance. The solar cycle became a daily exemplar of miraculous rebirth, which enabled Ra to bring light to his people.

Shiva Nataraja

The image of Shiva as Lord of the Dance reminds Hindus of the unending process of creation and destruction.

SACRED CALENDARS

We are often aware of the apparently chaotic pace of our lives, in which artificial demarcations of time, such as appointments, deadlines and weekends, have replaced the natural patterns of the seasons and of night and day. Great seasonal festivals were central to all ancient cultures, marking a year's progression from spring regeneration to winter stasis and motivated by thanksgiving, celebration, propitiation or penance. Even today, our religious festivals retain underlying associations with the year's cycle. Increasingly shielded from the elements, we need these rituals to sustain our spiritual focus and an understanding of our role in the natural world.

Everywhere across the globe, spring festivals are primarily joyous occasions, as winter's hold over the land is broken. This was traditionally a time when temples and homes were ritually cleansed and the demons of the old year expelled, sometimes by a scapegoat who would assume and bear away the sins and evils of the community. Several of the customs in modern religious festivals are pagan in origin: Christian spiritual regeneration at Easter, for example, is linked with the egg, a potent symbol of rebirth, resurrection and fertility. Many local customs involving eggs took place at Easter, such as painting, dyeing or even trundling, in which brightly coloured eggs were rolled down hills. In Teutonic myth, the egg was laid by the Easter Hare, a creature whose origins may be found in the sacrificial animal dedicated to Eostre (the goddess of spring, from whom Easter derived its name). The Hindu festival of Holi, which originally celebrated the growing crops, is one of India's most popular festivals – streets become alive with riotous colour as participants, dressed in dazzling clothes and jewellery, throw coloured water or pigments at each other.

Midsummer was often a time for fire festivals, when the Sun, after climbing higher and higher in the sky, began to retrace its steps. At the summer solstice bonfires invoked sympathetic magic to encourage the Sun to hold on to its power. In a variation on the custom, huge wheels of fire were sent hurtling down mountain sides, or wheels of flame were shot into the air from high places. At the Celtic fire festivals of Beltane (spring), Lughnasa (late summer) and Samhain (autumn), people also lit huge bonfires on the tops of mountains and hills.

Autumn is traditionally a time to celebrate the completion of the year's work: the first fruits of the harvest were offered to deities or spirits or to the souls of ancestors before feasting could begin. Plants were often believed to have souls, which required propitiation when the crop was first cut. In ancient times autumn festivals celebrated the dying gods of vegetation, such as the Egyptian Osiris and the Babylonian Tammuz (see page 82). Weeping, wailing, beating breasts and tearing hair were part of the rituals enacted in mourning for the sacrificed sheaves of corn.

Totem Poles
This totem pole from a British Columbian village portrays the sacred ancestral beings of the tribe. In great seasonal festivals, such as the Lakota Sun Dance, totem poles were believed to provide channels for the power of ancestors and spirits.

A Christian Book of Hours
The "canonical hours" of the Roman Catholic Church are the seven daily times of prayer. The set prayers or offices were sometimes contained in highly illustrated volumes such as the Forester Book of Hours *featured here. Books of Hours guided their wealthy readers through the devotions of the Christian year.*

Light is a highly evocative spiritual symbol, and is a particular feature of ceremonies conducted in the depths of winter. Almost universally, light represents the power of new or enduring life, offering protection against the forces of darkness. Divali is celebrated in Hindu tradition by placing candles in the windows of homes and temples; small boats, made from coconut shells or leaves, carry candles down the waterways, and children run about the streets lighting fireworks. The Jewish festival of Hanukkah commemorates the historic re-dedication of the Temple in Jerusalem, after it had been recaptured in a revolt from Greek rulers who had erected an altar to Zeus on the site. In their re-dedication ceremony, the Jews used their last available consecrated oil to light the candles.

The oil miraculously lasted eight days, an event joyously celebrated each year in the ritual lighting of the Menorah, the sacred candlestick (see page 156).

Seasonal festivals are still times when people turn aside from personal concerns and unite as a community. Transcending their feelings of powerlessness and the fear of elemental forces, the ritual prayers, music and dance enable participants to share in the rapture and victory of the gods.

Divali – Festival of Lights
The Hindu festival of Divali is held on the moonless night that concludes the month of Ashvina (usually late October or early November). Families invite Lakshmi, the goddess of prosperity, into their homes, hoping that she will bring luck for the year ahead.

SACRED SKIES

Even in our technological century, we can still feel humbled by the vastness and mystery of the night sky. Since earliest times, people have believed the star-studded vault of night to represent the entrance to another cosmic realm – sometimes the eventual resting-place of our souls, often thought to fly upward from the body after death; sometimes the impenetrable home of the gods who govern human existence. As we gather more scientific data about the stars and planets of our galaxy, we realize how much still eludes us in trying to comprehend the cosmos in which we live.

A Cree Image of the Moon
Most cultures view the Moon as female, but hunting societies – such as the Native American Cree, who often trap animals at night – may see the Moon as a male deity.

The first communities, observing the movements of the Sun and Moon, were aware that the relationship between Earth and sky affected every part of their existence. Rituals celebrated the year's changing seasons and reinforced sacred links between the heavens and the Earth. Even today, the dates of many holy festivals, such as Passover, Easter, Holi and the Islamic fasting month of Ramadan, are all determined by an ancient lunar calendar, and may fall upon different dates – even, in the case of Ramadan, at different seasons – in each solar year.

Early people's astonishingly accurate knowledge of celestial patterns is demonstrated by the precise alignment of Neolithic stone structures, such as Callanish in Lewis, Scotland, and Stonehenge in southern England, with the positions of the Sun and Moon at key moments in the year. At Newgrange, an Irish passage-grave dating from *c*.3000 BCE, the rays of the rising Sun stream over the threshold at dawn on the winter solstice, illuminating the central chamber and altar stone. The great Mayan city of Chichén Itzá, built *c*.600–830 CE, contains an elaborate observatory orientated toward several astronomical events: the rising and setting of the Sun at the equinoxes; the setting of the Pleiades; and the recurring appearance and disappearance of the planet Venus – the Mayan god Kukulcan.

The Babylonians divided the sky into 36 sections – three "roads", each containing 12 star gods. Later, they identified 12 zodiac constellations, which subsequently formed the basis of the Greek zodiac along the ecliptic (the apparent annual path of the Sun around the Earth). This ecliptic-based system was central to the development of Western astrology and astronomy, and is still in use today.

The most conspicuous bodies in the sky are the Sun and Moon, to which every culture has attached sacred importance. The Moon came to be perceived as female and the Sun as male – usually the divine father or eye of the world. To the Aztecs, the Sun was a bloodthirsty god

The Ascent of Elijah

In the Hebrew Bible, great events are often heralded by unusual weather conditions. This Russian icon depicts a whirlwind propelling the Prophet Elijah upward in a chariot and horses of fire.

whose divine power was being constantly burnt up; he demanded replenishment through the daily sacrifice of human hearts and blood (see page 62). The Moon, with its phases of dark and light, symbolizes the rhythm of cosmic cycles and, in human terms, of death and rebirth.

To early peoples the movements of Sun, Moon and major planets against the network of stars were symbolic of heavenly order and harmony, to which the individual soul was profoundly linked. Astrology, one of the oldest systems of divination, interprets meaning from the positions of the Sun, Moon and visible planets, with the Earth providing a central reference point. The chart for an individual is cast at the moment of birth, when the

psychological potential of new life becomes synchronized with celestial relationships. For thousands of years, astrology was an accepted feature of life: no wars were fought, treaties signed, or marriages arranged, until skies were scanned for good or bad omens.

Weather conditions were also thought to reflect the state of harmony on Earth. In China the mandate of the Emperor's rule was called in question by evil omens in the sky. Thunder represents in many cultures the voice and weapon of male sky gods, such as Thor and Zeus. The immense power of the thunderbolt, or *vajra*, gave its name to Vajrayana Buddhism, the later flowering of the Buddha's teachings in Tibet and the Far East.

THE WORLD OF ILLUSION

As human beings, we all share a need to understand our soul's relationship with the universe, and to see beyond the limitations and confusions of our individual lives. In modern, secular cultures spiritual meanings may become diminished or obscured by the pressures to achieve material success. We may feel that we now inhabit an "unreal" world, in which science and commerce have alienated us from the natural environment and distorted an ancient awareness of our true place in the cosmos.

Ancient Greek philosophers, such as Plato, Socrates and Aristotle, were the first to link the nature of the soul with a radical exploration of illusion and reality. In Plato's highly influential writings, true reality was perceived to lie in the realm of "ideas" or "forms" that can be understood by our reason – rather than in the world of the senses, where everything flows and nothing is permanent. This world of ideas, which draws upon the mathematician Pythagoras's belief in an abstract, harmonious realm of numbers, contains the eternal patterns behind the fleeting appearances of the mundane world. The realm of ideas informs all sensual experience: a black dog, for example, derives its form from the universal idea of a dog and the universal idea of blackness. Plato's philosophical vision also carries a profound spiritual charge: the human soul yearns to return to its true origins in this realm, and to escape from the constraints of a physical body.

To illustrate his theory, Plato described an underground cave in which chained prisoners faced the rear wall, unable to turn around to see the daylight. Behind them a fire was burning, and between the fire and the prisoners was a path, along which people passed, carrying all sorts of objects. These objects cast a variety of dancing shadows on to the wall of the cave – and the prisoners, who had never seen any other reality except this, imagined that the shadows were the real world.

Can we trust our senses? Is the world as it seems to be? Is there any way to see beyond the reality presented through our senses? Such profound questions have dominated the traditions of philosophy and spirituality in both East and West. They continue to preoccupy us today, in religious traditions, in mystical experiences and in certain psychological theories, such as those of Carl Jung. According to Jung's beliefs, dreams may represent a state in which the soul seeks to return to an ultimate reality, expressed through a language of intuitive symbols.

The imagery of philosophical poems or stories is often more successful than argument in expressing ideas about reality and illusion. A story by the Daoist philosopher Zhuang Zhou shows how bewildering the soul's search for true identity can be. "Once Zhuang Zhou dreamed

Plato's Cave of Shadows
Plato taught that we should keep our minds and hearts open to the possibility of higher realities, rather than relying on our five senses for information.

Zhuang Zhou's Butterfly Dream
The Book of Zhuang Zi, *written by Zhuang Zhou in the 3rd century* BCE, *uses the philosophical questions posed by a dream to encourage readers to reassess their true identities.*

that he was a butterfly, fluttering over the flowers, not knowing that he was Zhuang Zhou. Suddenly he woke with a start and was Zhuang Zhou again. However, although he was awake he did not know if he was Zhuang Zhou dreaming that he was a butterfly, or a butterfly dreaming that he was Zhuang Zhou."

Whereas the philosopher tries to pin down reality through conceptual thought, spiritual traditions look for ways of experiencing it directly. One of the principal statements from the *Dao De Jing* says that the *Dao* (Way) is by definition unfathomable: "The *Dao* which can be spoken is not the true *Dao*, the name which can be uttered is not the eternal name. Without a name it is the beginning of Heaven and Earth; with a name it is the Mother of all things." In Daoism, the ideal is *wu wei*, non-doing or non-action, which is not intent upon any result. If the individual soul is in harmony with reality, the mind can return to original clarity, stillness, tranquillity, silence: the perfect *Dao*. The flickering shadows of sense perceptions may then be seen against the backdrop of this immense and absolute stillness.

A Daoist Monk Meditating
Daoist meditation aims to empty the mind of thoughts that are distorted by an individual's consciousness. This 13th-century Chinese woodblock features Sima Chengzhen, an 8th-century master.

ILLUSION AND EGO

Those who follow spiritual beliefs do not view philosophical enquiry as an end in itself: it is simply one of many ways to help us recognize that the satisfaction of appetites may not be the only valid focus of our existence, and to help us explore more challenging avenues. In many religions this is accompanied by the acknowledgment that preoccupation with our individual selves is part of the complex of illusions that we must discard.

Freedom from the demands of the ego is the primary spiritual goal of most Eastern religions, and the means by which *moksha*, or release from the unending cycle of rebirth (see page 20), may be found. In Hinduism, every action in the world has consequences which either bind an individual soul more closely to the world of illusion or enable it to move nearer to an ideal of virtuous, disinterested detachment. The Jain religion similarly seeks a withdrawal from the world, achieved through disciplines of mental and physical austerity, while an essential tenet of Buddhism is the premise of enlightenment through negation of egotism. As the Buddha himself observed, "Just as the great oceans have but one taste, so too there is but one taste fundamental to all true teachings of the way and this is the taste of freedom."

The progress toward such spiritual liberation is exemplified by events described within the Buddha's own life. He was born Prince Siddhartha in a region of northern India, and spent his early life in a palace, surrounded by every form of luxury and sensual delight. However, Siddhartha managed as a young man to escape into the world outside the palace, in which he confronted the shocking decay of old age, the agony of sickness and the finality of death. Realizing that his pleasurable life had been illusory, Siddhartha became consumed by the desire to find meaning in the trials of human existence. For many years he became a wandering ascetic, subjugating his body to enable his soul to transcend the physical world. Yet the path of self-mortification did not lead to the true wisdom he desired.

Eventually Siddhartha came to rest under what is known as the Bodhi Tree, vowing not to leave that place until either his understanding was complete or he died. In the quietness of the night, he reflected upon the perpetual motion of the wheel of life, recognizing that present experience was caused by past actions in a process called karma. He perceived that false adherence to the ego prompted a terrible chain reaction: in trying to defend an illusory sense of self, people continued to be ignorant of their true nature and were consequently brought to suffer again and again. He recognized that he too had been caught up in the search for egotistical security, but that the projections to which his mind had clung were insubstantial. Like clouds in the sky they appeared and disappeared, arising from and dissolving into space. When Siddhartha had this realization, he touched the ground and called the Earth to witness his spiritual release from the illusory world of *samsara*, the endless cycle of rebirth (see page 20). At that moment he became Buddha, the awakened one.

The Bodhi Tree
Bodh Gaya, the site of the Bodhi Tree under which the Buddha gained enlightenment, is today one of the holiest of Buddhist sites.

The Armies of Mara attacking Prince Siddhartha

The demon Mara, sensing that Siddhartha was about to achieve enlightenment, sent his armies to oust him from his place beneath the Bodhi Tree. Siddhartha remained unmoved.

The insights that the Buddha gained during the night at the Bodhi Tree became the essence of his teaching on the Four Noble Truths (see page 149). The reality of the physical world was concentrated in the concept of *duhkha*, a word meaning suffering but also carrying the implications of impermanence, imperfection and lack of satisfaction. *Duhkha* could be escaped only by transcending egotism and achieving true enlightenment. The Buddha believed that the path to attaining this transcendence was accessible to ordinary people, but that the mind had to be in "a state of wisdom" to comprehend it. In common with other religions of the East, as well as some Western mystical traditions, the Buddha believed that attempts to capture spiritual truth in written form were bound to fail. Ultimate reality could only be grasped through the power of symbol: words, according to the Buddha, merely offered pointers toward truth. In one of his most famous sermons at Vulture Peak Mountain, in front of thousands of people, the Buddha sat in silence and simply held up a flower.

PANTHEONS OF THE GODS

The Pantheon of Ancient Greece
The ancient Greeks believed that their lives and destinies were governed by a number of gods and goddesses, who each had their own sphere of influence. This relief from Brauron, near Athens, shows the supreme god Zeus (sitting) with three of his children: Athene, the goddess of wisdom; Apollo, the god of healing, poetry and music; and Artemis, the goddess of hunting.

For many of us, the life of the soul is linked with our chosen religion. We look to sacred texts and rituals for a better understanding of the essential truths that both inform and transcend our world. Patterns of worship vary widely between different systems of belief, as do the manifestations that divine power assumes – sometimes human form, sometimes animal, sometimes aspects of both. Yet, for all their differences, faiths share a common purpose: to open our eyes to the reality of the divine.

Most of the world's great religions divide into monotheistic and pantheistic systems of belief. Some focus upon the existence of a single divine power; others are structured around one supreme being with many different aspects; yet others encompass the worship of a large number of gods and goddesses. Where no "official"

interpretation of religious belief existed, as in the Celtic world, thousands of individual cults developed, venerating similar deities under bewilderingly diverse names and aspects. Even in more formalized faiths, there exist many variations on the orthodox interpretation. An educated priest may be aware that the many forms of a deity are expressions of one transcendent power, but the ordinary worshipper continues to supplicate particular gods and goddesses in their familiar and well-loved forms.

The vast and ancient Hindu religion has evolved a highly complex pantheon. Its multiplicity of gods and goddesses are all manifestations of the supreme power of *brahman* – a pure consciousness, beyond concepts and forms, whose authority pervades and dominates the cosmos. Yet individual Hindu gods are worshipped in an extraordinarily wide variety of forms. Shiva, for example, is simultaneously revered as the Lord of the Dance who represents and controls the harmonious movements of the universe (see page 21); as the naked and dishevelled god of asceticism, garlanded with skulls and frequenting charnel grounds; and as the creative force of male sexual energy (see page 53). The other two principal deities are Brahma the Creator and Vishnu the Preserver, the latter well known for his many avatars, or incarnations, who intervene beneficially in the human world. The heroic Rama and Krishna, respectively the seventh and eighth avatars of Vishnu, are the god's most popular forms. The ninth avatar of Vishnu is believed by Hindus to be the Buddha, despite certain doctrinal conflicts between Buddhism and Hinduism.

The gods and goddesses of early religions tend to have been recognized as individual powers, not related to one higher deity, but retaining their own sphere of influence. They were often linked to the forces of the elements and the regenerative cycles of the seasons. Unconcerned with morality or ethics, and largely indifferent to the sufferings of humankind, these divinities were worshipped for their power. The sophisticated religions of the ancient Greeks and Romans also featured deities whose intervention lacked a consistent moral imperative. Instead, they epitomized contradictory features of the human psyche: sexual love, jealousy, delight in war and conflict, serenity and wisdom, roguish trickery and casual, roving lust.

The three major Western religions – Judaism, Christianity and Islam – affirm the same fundamental doctrine that there is only one, omnipotent God. These

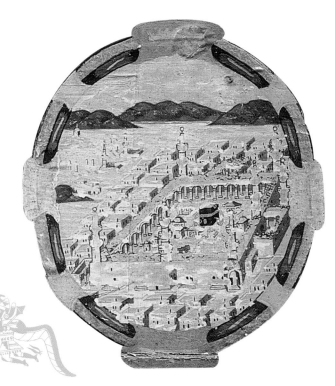

The Ka'bah Within the Great Mosque at Mecca
This detail from a 9th-century Koran shows the Ka'bah, Islam's holiest shrine, which is used for the exclusive worship of Allah.

monotheistic religions perceive time and history as linear and finite, rather than cyclical (see page 20), and have in common the conviction that God made himself known to his chosen followers through a form of special revelation – be it the holy teachings given to the Jews in the Torah, or the preaching and ministry of Christ, or the sacred words of the Koran. All three religions share the same root texts and the same ancient mythology, and acknowledge the holiness of the city of Jerusalem. They also believe in a divine antithesis: a powerful spirit of evil, personified by Satan, the fallen angel of light.

BALANCING HEAVEN AND EARTH

Many of us experience deep spiritual feelings in a natural environment, surrounded by the beauty of flowers, trees and birdsong. In tending our gardens or admiring the countryside, we recognize and celebrate the sacredness of our physical world. Nature's abundance reveals a harmonious balance of Earth and the heavens that nourishes the wellbeing of the individual soul.

The indigenous religion of Japan is Shinto – the so-called "Way of the *kami*", or gods. A pantheistic religion, Shinto recognizes a multiplicity of deities produced from the primal union of a divine brother and sister, Izanagi and Izanami, on the "floating bridge of heaven". *Kami* are essentially divine spirits who enter the world and imbue it with sacred life. As the expression and affirmation of a revered and animate universe, the *kami*'s presence is closely associated with the rituals and activities of daily existence. This extends in one instance to divine parentage – the Japanese imperial family traces its descent from the powerful Sun goddess Amaterasu, although the Emperor no longer claims to be a living god.

Kami are essentially guardian spirits of the land, linked to the elements (especially storms and wind), natural features – the Moon, rivers, lakes, trees and rocks – and agriculture. The rice goddess, for example, is petitioned annually for assistance with the growing and harvesting of her crop. Like Amaterasu, she has a shrine at the highly sacred Ise complex, which is destroyed and rebuilt every 20 years. Shinto's close connection with nature and fertility ensures the popularity of the religion's ceremonies at weddings, in contrast to the predominance of the Buddhist faith at many Japanese funerals.

Ikebana

Shinto, the native Japanese religion, teaches a reverence for all natural things. This philosophy was adopted by practitioners of ikebana, who arrange flowers as a means of expressing their spiritual ideals.

Shrines and temples become extremely important in a localized religion without traditional scriptures or rigid doctrines. Shinto worshippers prefer simple shrines, located at sacred sites and entered through formal gateways known as *torii*. An intuitive need to communicate directly with the *kami* often resists ornate decoration, and the shrines, placed amid trees and gardens and containing pure water in stone troughs, underscore the relation of human beings to the natural world.

Yet *kami* are not solely nature spirits, a fact that has enabled Shinto to retain its influence in a modern, industrialized Japan. They are associated with the arts, leisure activities and even industries. Shinto priests are often invited to honour the *kami* of a new business location or a manufacturing site. Such reverence is believed to channel cosmic energy into the enterprise, through divine intervention and support.

Kami maintain a domestic presence too. A "god shelf" in the home supports daily offerings of salt, rice and water, inviting the divine spirit to participate in, and bring harmony to, the rituals of cleaning, washing and eating that characterize everyday family life. This balance between secular and divine is not unique to Shinto, however; other cultures have honoured the spirits of the household and farm in similar ways. Roman

The Shinto Gateway to the Gods

In Japan, to enter the precinct of a Shinto shrine, a worshipper must first pass under the torii. *This ceremonial gate represents the threshold separating the secular world from the sacred world of the* kami *(gods).*

homes, for example, contained shrines dedicated to the *Lares*, ancient household gods associated with the family's prosperity. In modern Bali, religion is integrally linked to every aspect of daily life, and curious rituals, such as the honouring of cars, bicycles and metal tools, express a profound veneration of the quotidian world.

Shinto is very much a personal religion, which finds communal expression in *matsuri* – regional festivals in honour of the *kami*, who may be transported around their local area in a portable shrine. Such ceremonies are joyous, reflecting Shinto's vitality and relevance as a "life religion" that links spirituality with the physical world.

DIVINATION

All of us have wished on occasion to be able to predict the future and discover the significance of patterns of incident, such as recurring encounters or dreams, that we may recognize in our own lives. Divination uses a symbolic key to decipher the underlying meaning of physical forms, such as the progress of the heavens or the movements of animals or birds. Knowledge of the future and manifestations of divine will have been sought in many strange guises, including the entrails of sacrificed animals, markings produced by oil or molten lead on water, configurations of smoke from burning incense, and cloud formations. The principle behind divination, known as synchronicity, recognizes an essential link between inner and outer reality. We are not isolated beings but part of a unified cosmos, and great wisdom can be found through analyzing the apparently random phenomena of the physical world.

In China the clarity that came from divination was called the "light of the gods", and brought the individual soul into harmony with the cosmos. This essential unity lies at the heart of the *Yi Jing* ("The Book of Changes"), the oldest complete divinatory system to survive from the ancient world. Its core text dates from well before 1500 BCE and contains the roots of both Daoism and Confucianism. The *Yi Jing* uses sticks made from yarrow plant stems to compose up to 64 hexagons that reflect all structures within a perpetually moving universe. The dynamic interaction between complementary pairs of opposites is believed to create images that mirror the structure of the human psyche. In ancient China divination provided an access to the cosmic forces shaping a particular moment of time, and enabled skilled individuals to interpret the future.

Divination Plate
Many practices of divination involve throwing objects upon a chart and interpreting the pattern that is formed when they fall. In Nigeria, diviners make predictions from the shapes made by rice or seeds on special plates.

Shamanic practices of divination are focused upon direct encounter with the spirit world. The Native American Ojibway people enact their sacred summoning ceremonies in a divination lodge known as "Shaking Tent" – a barrel-like structure, around 7 feet (2 metres) in height and covered with bark, canvas or skins. The shaman invokes his or her personal guardian spirits, or *pawagonak*. He or she may also summon assistance from the souls of the dead and the spirits of the natural world. The arrival of the spirits of the winds causes the tent to shake, and strange songs uttered by the spirit voices signal the start of the divination process.

Oracles have been an important feature of divination in the early civilizations of both East and West. Often

Tarot Cards
One of the best-known forms of divination in the West uses Tarot cards. The questioner shuffles the cards, after which the diviner spreads them face down in a certain way and then turns them over one by one. Each of the cards represents an archetype or image, which reveals something about the questioner. Together, the cards form a pattern of past, present and future feelings and events which can then be interpreted by the diviner.

located near symbolic physical features, such as caves, springs or rock clefts, they offered channels of communication with the gods or spirits. Highly respected and often sacred mediators engaged in dialogue with the gods, sometimes through utterances and movements produced in an ecstatic trance. At the famous Delphic oracle in Greece, the prophecies of the Pythia, the oracle's priestess, are thought to have been inspired by strong vapours emerging from a rock crevice. Questions put to oracles ranged from major political dilemmas – whether to wage war or to join an alliance – to simple domestic concerns. In taking counsel from an oracle, an individual sought to act in harmony with the governing principles of both physical and spiritual worlds.

The Tibetans practise many forms of divination. Before Chinese control was established, the State Oracle was a paid government official whose national duty involved entering into trance states to talk with the gods. Another celebrated Tibetan method of divination, known as *prasena*, enabled the unconscious mind to project visionary images onto the surface of a mirror.

Scientific materialism, often dismissive of divination, has still to resolve the vast complexities of cause and effect. The physicist Werner Heisenberg has observed that in examining nature and the universe, "man encounters himself" rather than finding objective truth. Science may yet come to support the ancient belief that our universe possesses a complex, intelligent structure, upon which the human psyche ultimately depends.

SACRED SPACE

In visiting sacred places, whether of the present or the past, we often experience a distinct spiritual charge. These are the points of the Earth most closely connected with the gods, and separated from the mundane world by physical or intuitive boundaries. The divine presence that we sense in such places – sometimes with a feeling almost of fear – is often reinforced by architecture and decoration that reflect our aspirations toward the heavens.

A sacred place requires a clear spiritual focus and separation from its physical surroundings. The word "temple" (and the associated activity of contemplation) originates from the Latin *templum*, meaning a piece of land marked off from ordinary uses and dedicated to a god. The structures and orientation of sacred buildings provide expressions of, rather than merely a shell for, numinous experience. Their architecture must attempt to capture the divine presence and reveal it to the individual worshipper,

Stupas
Stupas *are dome-shaped monuments that are believed to house the bodily relics of the Buddha and his prominent disciples. Their sacred architecture is believed to represent the Buddha's path to liberation.*

Temple of Amun at Karnak
The vast Egyptian temple at Karnak is dedicated to Amun, the creator god. The temple's pillars are carved with papyrus flowers, evoking the Egyptian creation myth of a primordial island that remained after flood waters had receded.

together with the recognition that a transcendent deity is infinitely greater than any physical site. The dome of an Islamic mosque or a Christian cathedral directs the worshipper's gaze toward the heavens and the inexpressible majesty of God. Many Christian Orthodox churches feature the Byzantine interpretation of Christ Pantocrator – Ruler of All Things – (see page 142) inside the central dome or the apse. The dominant, highly stylized image depicts Christ, in the words of a Byzantine writer, "looking down from the rim of heaven", one hand raised in the gesture of divine blessing. The all-knowing, implacable visage of the Pantocrator combines Christ's cosmic omnipotence with his role as universal judge – the fate of the individual soul and the harmony of Creation are thus profoundly and inextricably linked. The curve of the dome surrounds the viewer with the awe and immediacy of divine encounter, describing through physical image the miraculous incarnation in which God became human flesh.

Neither synagogues nor mosques contain any representations of the deity; divine authority is revealed instead through the venerated word. The Ark containing the holy scrolls of the Jewish Torah is the focus of all synagogue rituals, and is always set into the wall facing the Temple Mount in Jerusalem. In Islam, the perfection of Allah is manifested through the elaborate calligraphy on

The Temple of Heaven
Reflecting Confucian belief, the ceiling of the Hall of Prayer for Good Harvest in the Temple of Heaven, Beijing, reproduces the geometric structure of heaven.

the walls of the mosque – inscriptions from the Koran suspended in aesthetic abstraction beyond space and time. The intricate patterning of mosaics, such as those in the magnificent dome of the Lutfullah Mosque in Isfahan, Iran, is both harmonious and mesmerizing, charged with spiritual meaning. As the dome spreads outward, geometric patterns represent the interwoven ordering of Creation around a central, omnipotent God.

In contrast, Hindu temples provide a more literal dwelling-place for the individual deity, who is believed to reside within the sculpted image usually located in the innermost sanctuary. Worship is manifested through daily rituals of waking, dressing, bathing and feeding this image, and even providing the shrine with couches and curtains to enable the divine presence to rest in privacy.

A classic Hindu temple includes a rising tower above the inner sanctuary, symbolizing Mount Meru, the axis of the spiritual universe (see page 19). The ground plan, in the form of a *mandala*, represents both a map of the cosmos and the soul's progress through meditation toward enlightenment. The Buddhist temple at Angkor in Cambodia embodies this spiritual symbolism: the central kingdom of Jampudvipa (the human realm) is encircled by six rings of mountain ranges and seven oceans, and the sacred Mount Meru is set in the exact centre.

Different cultures have always sought to live close to their gods, and to reinforce links between physical and spiritual worlds. The spire of a cathedral, the minaret of a mosque and the Buddhist *stupa* all emphasize the subordination of earthly existence to the life of the soul.

CELESTIAL REALMS

The beauty and magnitude of the heavens have fascinated our imagination from the earliest times. Studded with stars, planets, the Sun and the Moon, the immense revolving vault of sky symbolizes the soul's transcendence of the material world. Many systems of belief have interpreted the movement of heavenly bodies as the divine actions of gods and goddesses, and looked to the signs of the zodiac to foretell the future. Exceptional events, such as a solar or lunar eclipse or the appearance of a flaming comet, were often believed to have terrifying consequences on Earth. Many forms of sacred architecture seek to mirror the patterns of the heavens, in order to strengthen the spiritual bond between gods and the Earth.

The Great Bear
This Chinese image shows the Great Bear constellation, believed in some cultures to represent the energy that created the universe.

Amaterasu
The Sun goddess Amaterasu has ruled the Shinto pantheon since vanquishing her brother Susano. Her retreat into a cave during this conflict brought the world darkness and misery until she re-emerged.

Comets
Alien intruders in the cosmos have traditionally been viewed with unease as portents of famine, pestilence or war. Comets, with their streaming fiery tails, were often thought to be expressions of divine wrath, particularly of the Sun gods. Their infrequent presence among the more ordered movement of the heavens threatened the delicate equilibrium, causing related disturbances in the human realm.

The Chariot of the Sun

The Temple of the Sun at Konarak in India was built in honour of Surya, the Sun god, in the 13th century. Its structure represents the flaming chariot that he drove across the heavens, and 12 enormous stone chariot wheels (above) stand outside the main entrance. The cyclical concept of time that underlies Indian spiritual beliefs is symbolized by these vast wheels; it is also mirrored in the daily solar cycle of departure and return.

A Chart of the Heavens

An Indian astrological chart of the 19th century, featuring the signs of the Eastern zodiac. Ancient Vedic texts interpreted movements of the "heavenly bodies", or jyotis, *determining the most auspicious time to conduct religious sacrifices.*

GODS

Jews, Christians and Muslims worship one God as the creator and ruler of the universe, the paternalistic controller and arbiter of human destiny. In pantheistic accounts there is often a supreme deity, who achieved his position by force of arms or through having created the other gods. In some myths, the supreme god is an abstract force – too remote and powerful for human conception – who withdrew out of reach after creating the universe. In contrast, gods of nature are tangible presences in an ensouled world, manifest in the local landscape, the elements, the strength and beauty of the animal realm and the mystery of the skies.

The Judeo-Christian God
In Genesis, God has human attributes, such as walking and talking. This painting of paradise (above), dating from the late 15th-century, shows him as a wise old man.

Odin
The Norse god Odin carried the spear of Tiwaz, which gave him control of battles. He sacrificed an eye to obtain knowledge.

Susano

The Shinto storm god Susano was the divine embodiment of disorder. He was expelled from heaven for trying to depose his sister Amaterasu. Susano is seen here with his wife, Kusa-nada-hime, whom he rescued from an eight-headed dragon.

Krishna

The eighth avatar of the Hindu god Vishnu, Krishna righted many wrongs and brought joy and love into the world. According to legend, he grew up in the countryside. This 18th-century painting shows him playing his enchanted flute, which he used to lure the gopis (cowherd girls) into the forest.

Amun-Ra

The greatest of the Egyptian gods, Amun-Ra was a combination of Amun and the Sun god Ra. In this powerful manifestation he was usually portrayed as a man crowned with two tall plumes, and was often referred to as "King of the gods".

GODDESSES

Our earliest ancestors, probably unaware of the male role in reproduction, viewed childbirth as a magical process. Linking the fertility of women with the fertility of the Earth, they worshipped a supreme deity, the Great Goddess, who gave, maintained and finally took back life. The Earth itself was often believed to be the body of the Goddess, and the changing seasons were seen as different aspects of her sacred nature. As humans changed from a migratory existence to a more stationary lifestyle, their societies became increasingly patriarchal and the status of the Goddess was gradually eroded. First she had a son or took a lover; then she was worshipped as the equal partner of a god; finally she was seen as the wife, mother, sister or daughter of a supreme god, or was demonized as a witch or monster. Today, echoes of the Great Goddess can be found world-wide. In China, Kwan-Yin is the generous and compassionate mother; in ancient Greece, Demeter is the fertility goddess who regulates the seasons, while the sensual Aphrodite controls love and sexuality; the Hindu Durga is a lethal avenger of wrongs; and the Christian Virgin Mary is the spotless queen of heaven.

Kwan-Yin
The goddess of mercy, especially toward women and children, Kwan-Yin was introduced to China by Buddhists as a bodhisattva, *or future buddha, who remains in this world to help others.*

Demeter
As the Greek goddess of fertility, Demeter was responsible for the productivity of the Earth. When her daughter, Persephone, was abducted by Hades, the lord of the underworld, Demeter went into mourning, causing the world to be barren for the winter months.

Selqet
This statue from the tomb of Tutankhamun is of Selqet, the Egyptian scorpion goddess. As the wife of the Sun god, Ra, she was a fertility goddess, presiding over childbirth and the family. She was also linked to the underworld and mummification.

The Virgin Mary

In the New Testament, Mary is a virgin when she is told by the Holy Ghost that she will be the mother of Jesus. Many Christians revere her for her immense suffering – she watched her son die on the cross.

Aphrodite

Love goddesses have traditionally been among the best known and frequently petitioned of a given pantheon. This bronze head of Aphrodite – the Greek goddess of love, renowned for her beauty, jealousy and faithlessness – dates from the 2nd or 1st century BCE.

Durga

Durga was the warrior aspect of the great Hindu Goddess Devi. One myth tells how Durga was created by the gods to destroy the demon Mahisha, who had grown too powerful and was threatening to take over the heavens. Durga annihilated Mahisha's army and then decapitated the demon. The goddess is usually depicted riding on a lion or tiger, symbols of her power.

The contrast between the finite existence of our physical bodies and the enduring life of the soul lies at the heart of many spiritual beliefs. In a material world, we are subject to the inexorable processes of ageing and death, but faith in the soul's

BODY AND SOUL

afterlife acknowledges these as the prelude to a far greater reality. The demands of our bodies in life, especially regarding sensual pleasures, are often considered antithetical to the spiritual perspective, and may be suppressed in extreme acts of renunciation and aestheticism. However, other religious traditions consider our bodies to be essential vehicles of divine worship. Through the ecstatic sexual union of Tantric belief, or the sacred actions of supplication, dance, pilgrimage and sacrifice, devotees transcend the physical world to approach and celebrate the spiritual.

THE SOUL IN THE BODY

In recent times there has been an unprecedented obsession in the West with youth and physical beauty. This has coincided with an equally strong decline in religious faith and practice. Many believe that by abandoning our spiritual values and worshipping the physical, we have created a damagingly narcissistic culture, which could prove fatal. As a society we have neglected the relationship between the physical body, with its instinctive demands and gradual degeneration, and the needs of the soul. Yet this relationship is an important ingredient in all human systems of belief.

Early civilizations revered the regenerative power of the natural world, and the human body provided an appropriate vehicle of worship. The never-ending cycle of the seasons, and the associated rhythms of life and death, were celebrated in ritual dances and hunts, sacrifices and fertility rites. Physical actions were often re-enacted in religious ceremonies to express the achievement of a spiritual state. For example, the Celts in Cornwall, England, symbolically enacted their spiritual rebirth by climbing through the hole in a sacred stone, the Men-an-tol or Crick Stone near Morvah.

Later religious traditions often viewed the body as impure and inferior to the soul. Plato taught that the soul belonged to a constant world of ideas, to which it longed to return throughout its earthly existence (see page 26). To achieve release, the individual should resist the body's contaminating influence, and focus upon a transcendent spiritual ideal. If a person gave in to bodily passions and pleasures, the soul could not escape from the material world and would be reborn in gross animal form.

The early Christians drew upon other faiths, including Gnosticism and Manichaeism, for many of their views on the body, which often varied significantly from the images used by Christ. Gnostic doctrines, which flourished until the 4th century CE, believed in a sharp dichotomy between a corrupt, material world and the realm of the spirit. An individual soul could achieve freedom in death through the generation of *gnosis*, the

Donna flagellata e baccante danzante
Pain, whether self-inflicted or received at the hand of another, can induce a change in consciousness. Flagellation, depicted in this 1st-century BCE Roman mural from the Villa dei Misteri in Pompeii, was part of the orgiastic rites of the Roman god Bacchus.

light of divine wisdom. The founder of Manichaeism, Mani, preached across the Persian Empire in the 3rd century CE. He also taught that matter was evil, advocating asceticism and celibacy in the search for spiritual truth. Several early Christians, including St Augustine, were converts from Manichaeism and retained some of their old beliefs. Sex and lust were seen as synonymous, and the body's urges were viewed with fear or contempt.

Despite the Church's waning influence, its revulsion for the body has remained in our subconscious. Jung believed that revulsion masked a fear of losing control – the body was untrustworthy because it openly expressed emotions and demonstrated vulnerability by becoming weak and sick. Our residual ambivalence and insecurity about the body underlie most human experiences. Accepting the relationship of soul and body entails coming to terms with life's hardest lessons. However, the importance of this acceptance was stressed by the visionary poet William Blake, who declared in *The Marriage of Heaven and Hell*: "Man has no body distinct from his soul: for that called body is a portion of soul discerned by the five senses, the chief inlets of soul in this age."

Lilith

Originally a Sumerian wind goddess, Lilith features in Hebrew scriptures as a demonic queen. She was later said to be the first woman, who deserted her husband Adam. Lilith's evil influence on the male body was thought to cause men to ejaculate as they slept.

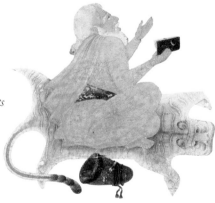

Raja Yoga

A practitioner of Raja Yoga, seen in this 16th-century miniature, rejects the body as an illusion. Knowledge and devotion are seen as the paths to release.

CHAKRAS AND MERIDIANS

Western science tends to see the body in physical terms, regarding it as a structure of blood, flesh and bone, and ignoring or denying the existence of the soul. However, some traditions, especially those of the East, believe that we all have a spiritual or "subtle" body that exists alongside the physical, and has its own energy. Tantric and Yogic disciplines attempt through meditation to release and harness this energy.

Just as the physical body is pervaded by the nervous system, so the subtle body is pervaded by thousands of channels *(nadi)* through which flow the winds of energy *(prana)*. These winds are believed to be as vital to our existence as food or water. The central channel runs from the crown of the head to the base of the spine, and along it are seven focal points known as *chakras* (energy wheels). As the *chakras* revolve, they initiate secondary energy flows, which circulate through the physical body along the meridians – a network of energy channels that can be accessed through acupuncture.

In most people, just enough energy flows through the *chakras* to sustain life. However, in meditation, the practitioner concentrates on bringing the energy winds together at the base of the spine and then carrying them up through the *chakras*, thus unlocking emotional and spiritual energy that has been blocked.

The first three *chakras* are connected to individual qualities. The first, called the "Root Support", at the base of the spine is linked with security and attachment to the earth. As this *chakra* unfurls, feelings of intense fear and insecurity may be created, but when it is fully open, these anxieties may be replaced by a true sense of unconditional trust. The second *chakra*, "Special Abode", is in the area of the genitals. Working with it releases sexual energy, which can be pleasurable, but also has destructive qualities. Self-confidence, optimism and creativity are all qualities linked to "Special Abode". The third *chakra* is positioned at the solar plexus. Known as "City of the Shining Jewel", it is associated with the achievement of goals and power. On opening, feelings of anger, constriction and frustration give way to spontaneity, expressiveness and decisiveness.

The middle two *chakras* are associated with communication. "Soundless Sound", the fourth *chakra*, is located at the heart and holds the power of love and compassion. The fifth, "Purification", at the throat, is linked to expression and creativity. Working with this centre can cause coughing as the liberated energy sends shock waves through the speech centre of the physical body.

The last two *chakras* are connected to realization. The sixth, "Command", is associated with understanding and vision and is located in-between the eyebrows. Profound disorientation may accompany the clearing of this *chakra*, as attachment to old ways of seeing dissolves. This confusion gives way to heightened perception and may also lead to extrasensory powers. The seventh *chakra* is the "Thousand-Petalled Lotus", the "Chakra of Great Bliss". It is said to be opened when the practitioner's individual energy and the energy of the cosmos are dissolved into one.

Chakras

A chakra is traditionally depicted as a wheel or petalled flower. Inside the circle, the chakra's essence is represented using symbols and inscriptions.

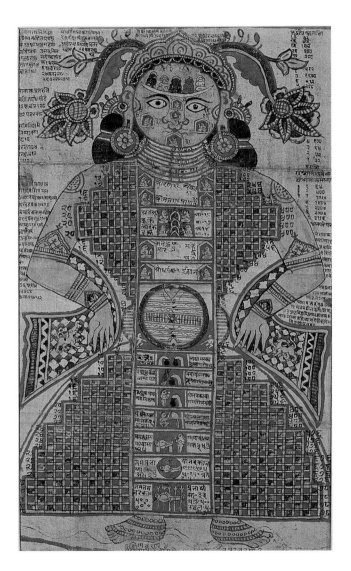

A Tantric Image of Cosmic Man
This 18th-century Rajasthani painting illustrates the link between the individual's energy and that of the cosmos. Levels of awareness and being are depicted along the central channel of the man's body.

Similar descriptions of the body and its subtle energy patterns are found in very different traditions around the world. Remarkably, they seem to have evolved independently of one another. In the Jewish mystical system of the Kabbalah, the centre of the Kabbalist's body was seen to be alive with knowledge. Seven spheres of heavenly power were located along the central channel. The left side of the channel was seen to be male, active and fiery, while the right side was female, receptive and watery. By combining the two qualities the disciple experienced the unifying principle of creation. The Inner Alchemy of the Daoists described the circulation of energies along the central column culminating in the great "Inner Union of Dragon and Tiger". Christian icons often include a halo or nimbus as a sign of divinity or sainthood, and this may represent the energetic aura believed by many to emanate from the enlightened.

The most complete descriptions of the *chakras* are found in Hindu Kundalini Yoga sources. Kundalini is the serpent energy that moves and illuminates life. In most people the serpent lies coiled and sleeping at the base of the central channel, but by practising yoga we can waken the serpent, so that it rises from the lowest to the highest levels, shaking off our spiritual lethargy and releasing both spiritual and physical energy. Frequent warnings have been given about the dangers of suddenly experiencing this energy. It is said that, without a skilful teacher, the student can become like a "drunk elephant", not knowing how to direct the energy in a positive direction. When correctly released, however, the great spiritual energy that we all possess can alter our perceptions and stimulate our progress toward enlightenment (see pages 156–7).

MALE AND FEMALE

In our struggle to make sense of ourselves and our world, we have often tried to explain or enact our feelings of isolation, separation and longing. Most of our creation myths tell how a single, total principle divided to form men and women, and many of the world's faiths contain an element of reunification, either physical or spiritual, that is a relic from a much older religion. Elemental forces have often been assigned gender and the rhythms of their union and separation linked to the pattern of the seasons, and the decay and regeneration of human life. Gender difference has gained spiritual importance as a primordial symbol of polarity – the creative power that exists between all dualisms in life and may be harmonious and complementary or conflicting and discordant.

This concept of polarity pervading the universe was expressed in the *Dao De Jing*, the revered Daoist classic, by the *yin-yang* symbol (see background image). The cosmic antitheses of female and male, night and day, Earth and sky, are held in a mutually dependent synthesis. Each side of the symbol contains within itself the seed of the other, bringing movement and change through their perpetual union and maintaining the harmony of the universe.

Plato believed that the transcendent union of male and female was reflected in the individual soul's search for a sexual partner. In his *Symposium*, the first beings each had eight limbs and were either male-male, male-

Hari-Hara

In Hindu myth, Hari-Hara is a combination of the two male gods Vishnu the Preserver (shown in blue) and Shiva the Destroyer (wearing a tiger skin).

female or female-female. They angered the god Zeus, who split them in two. Ever since, anguished humans have sought heterosexual or homosexual encounters in an attempt to reunite with their lost selves.

The Sun and the Moon have been the most enduring symbols of male and female polarity. The Sun has been viewed as male by many different belief systems. In ancient Egypt, the Sun god Ra was the supreme power at the heart of the cosmos (see page 21). Male Sun gods are invested with "masculine" attributes, such as great physical strength and prowess in battle. The Aztec Sun god Huitzilopochtli, for example, was also worshipped as the god of war, and conflict itself became a form of veneration for a civilization that linked its conquests to the victory of day over night.

By contrast, the Moon is often personified as female, symbolizing the rhythms of monthly change. Its cycle of appearance, growth and disappearance has been associated with the power of female Moon deities over birth, death and resurrection. Representing the dark, intuitive aspects of nature, she regulated tides, rain and the seasons. Because of the Moon's power over unpredictable forces, she was often portrayed as the controller of individual destinies and the weaver of human fate.

A complementary harmony between male and female principles was the goal of Western alchemy.

"Men Shall Know Nothing of This"
Alchemical references frequently appear in the work of the German artist Max Ernst. This painting, dating from 1923, portrays the divine copulation of the Sun and the Moon.

Phases of the Moon
Many systems of belief have related the cyclical waxing and waning of the Moon to the natural cycle of birth, growth and decay. The Moon became intimately linked with the powers of the Earth Goddess.

Symbolically the male was sulphur, depicted as red, solar, hot and active; while mercury was female – white, lunar, cold and passive. These two principles were set in conflict, to be reconciled by the skilful alchemist in the form of the Red King and White Queen. The philosopher's stone, the legendary key to enlightenment, was believed to derive from their union.

Such a reconciliation of opposites was often symbolized by the spiritual and sexual union of deities. Isis and Osiris, Dumuzi and Inanna, Shiva and Parvati are all examples of creative, powerful, divine partnerships. The *hieros gamos*, or sacred marriage, of the Greek god Zeus and his sister Hera was celebrated in rituals at Samos and Argos as the wedding of heaven and Earth. Polynesian mythology also features a divine marriage: Hawaiians traditionally worshipped rock formations that resembled paired male and female genitalia, believing them to symbolize the union of their ancestral gods.

The sacred marriage appears in transmuted form in Judeo-Christian belief. The biblical Song of Songs, which on the surface is a secular love poem, has been interpreted as a dialogue between either God and Israel or Jesus and the Church. The powerful image of Christ as the divine lover of the soul is reflected in the ecstatic visions of love mystics, such as St Bernard of Clairvaux and St Teresa of Avila (see page 146), who believed that the union was necessary to ensure the wellbeing of both body and soul, the material and spiritual worlds.

SEXUAL ENERGY

Shiva Linga
The linga *(phallus) is worshipped by Hindus as the incarnate form of the god Shiva. It is often shown set inside the* yoni *(vulva), as here.*

The sex drive is a primary physical instinct, integral to the survival of humankind. Its power and influence over our behaviour have been recognized by every culture. Sexuality has been considered both a distraction from, and a manifestation of, spiritual life. As an instinct shared by animals, some faiths have seen sex as a chain linking the soul to the material world; others have perceived erotic activity to be a vehicle of transcendence, and ecstasy an expression of the highest spiritual energy.

The creation of the cosmos is often explained by divine sexual union. Ancient Egyptian myths posited that the deities Osiris, Isis, Seth and Nepthys were born from the embrace of the Sky goddess Nut with the Earth god Geb. Vedic hymns describe the exploits of Prajapati (literally "the Lord of Progeny") who couples repeatedly with the Dawn to create the Earth's species. The sacred Shinto siblings, Izanagi and Izanami, produce children by uniting the "excessive" part of the male with the "insufficient" part of the female to form a perfect whole.

Early spiritual beliefs, structured around the natural cycles of death and regeneration, often included sexual activity as an aspect of worship. Human erotic energies were held to be sacred in many goddess-orientated religions, such as that of the Sumerian deity Inanna, whose sexual congress with the king Dumuzi was associated with the ploughing of the soil and the annual regeneration of crops. Sacred prostitutes featured in the religious traditions of ancient Greece, Rome and Mesopotamia. Considered to be manifestations of the goddess, they dwelt in the temples, offering male worshippers and initiates a mystical union with the divine.

The Lying Horse
This panel from a 19th-century Chinese scroll reveals the adoption of Daoist erotic techniques by the Mongols.

The paradoxical nature of the Hindu god Shiva, lord of asceticism and regeneration, is epitomized by the *linga* form in which he is worshipped. Erect yet never spilling seed, the *linga* (phallus) balances ascetic restraint with infinite procreative potential. The *linga* is usually set within a *yoni*, symbolizing the vulva and female energy, and forming a complementary union of antitheses.

Practitioners of Hindu Tantra may enter into ritual sexual congress to emulate the divine union of Shiva and the manifestation of the Goddess, Shakti. The passive and unknowable Shiva represents Perusa – the power of the spirit which animated the visible world while remaining hidden itself. In Buddhist Tantra, the male principle represents "skilful means" and the female principle wisdom. The *yab-yum* carvings of the deities found on Buddhist temples reveal a particular aspect of the body's enlightened energy, united with the wisdom of profound spiritual revelation.

Western monotheistic religions have generally regarded sexuality with suspicion or ambivalence. Both Judaism and Islam acknowledge the pleasures of sexual expression within marriage for the purposes of procreation, which may be interspersed with periods of ritual abstinence. The early Christian Church viewed indulgence in sensual pleasures as antithetical to spiritual purity, although paradoxically the divine covenant between Christ and believers is expressed on occasion in the New Testament through the image of the bridegroom bringing away his bride. Sex was perceived as essentially sinful and woman assumed the legacy of Eve as the instrument of sensual temptation. The entire female sex was condemned by the early Church father Tertullian as the *januas diaboli*, or devil's door.

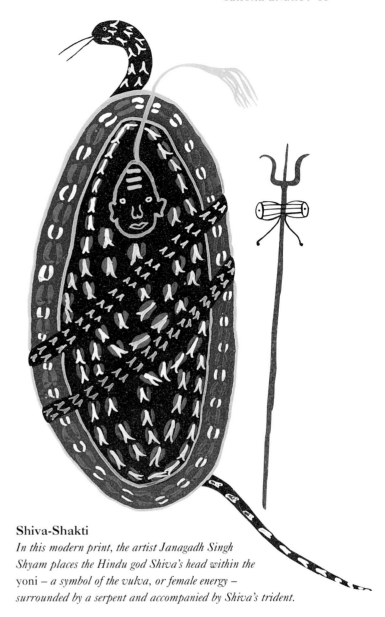

Shiva-Shakti
In this modern print, the artist Janagadh Singh Shyam places the Hindu god Shiva's head within the yoni – *a symbol of the vulva, or female energy – surrounded by a serpent and accompanied by Shiva's trident.*

Procreation in wedlock became the only permissible reason for sexual activity, and even that was viewed as inferior to celibacy by the more severe ascetics, such as St Paul and St Jerome. By its resistance and transcendence of the physical, the soul sought to overcome material obstacles and achieve a closer relationship with God.

PILGRIMAGE

There are times in our lives when we may feel that a physical journey to a sacred place – as an act of devotion, penance or thanksgiving, or to fulfil a vow – will further our spiritual development. Most world religions revere certain temples, cities or natural features because they are historically linked to their gods or prophets. Sometimes, as with Jerusalem, sites are important to more than one religion, perhaps suggesting that they have a fundamental, even intrinsic, sacredness. Buddhists and Jains visit the Ganges Basin, where both the historical Buddha and Mahavira, the Jain saint, lived, taught and died. The river Ganges itself is sacred to Hindus, and millions each year cleanse themselves in its waters, hoping to wash away their sins.

Some pilgrims, believing that their prayers are more likely to be heard if offered in a holy place, will journey hundreds of miles to make a specific request. During the Middle Ages, many thousands of Christians undertook pilgrimages to Jerusalem, Rome, Santiago de Compostela, Canterbury and Walsingham. Since then, other destinations such as Lourdes in France have gained a reputation for granting wishes or for healing.

Pilgrims at Kedarnath

The Hindu temple at Kedarnath is situated in the Himalayas, near the source of the Ganges. The river, temple and surrounding area are important pilgrimage sites for devotees of the god Shiva, who is believed to dwell in these mountains.

Certain religions demand that specific pilgrimages are undertaken by their worshippers. The last of the Five Pillars of Islam, for example, states that every Muslim who is physically able should journey to Mecca in Saudi Arabia at least once in his or her lifetime. The *hajj*, as this pilgrimage is called, is believed to bestow great merit and to wash away all sins.

Upon arrival in Mecca, the pilgrim enters a state of ritual purity, or *ihram*, by bathing and putting on two simple pieces of white cloth. Women wear additional garments to cover their legs and faces. The pilgrim then sets out for the Great Mosque. Throughout a Muslim's life, he or she will have prayed facing Mecca and now, in a sense, the pilgrim is approaching the journey's end, having travelled physically the route previously only followed by mind and heart. In the centre of the Great Mosque is the Ka'bah, a black shrine originally dedicated to pre-Islamic gods, but cleansed and re-dedicated by the Prophet Muhammad. It contains a black stone, possibly a meteorite, which some believe was found by Adam, the first man. The initial rite of the pilgrimage is

Scallop Shells

Pilgrims visiting St James's shrine at Compostela in Spain traditionally wore a scallop shell on their clothing. The shell was initially linked to the saint, but eventually became a general symbol of Christian pilgrimage.

the circumambulation: the devotee circles the Ka'bah seven times and at each circuit will try to kiss the black stone. The pilgrim then leaves the Great Mosque and journeys to the Plain of Arafat, where the Prophet gave his last sermon. Here, he or she stands in repentance on the Mount of Mercy, seeking release, cleansing and oneness with God. One of the final rites is the stoning of the three pillars at Mina, believed to represent Satan or the forces of evil. With each throw, the pilgrim hopes to destroy some of the shadows, temptations and evil impulses within his or her own heart.

Pilgrimage is the physical enactment of the journey to the source of sacredness. Pilgrims turn away from the teeming world of manifestation to the still point of the soul where all opposites are resolved. By travelling through unfamiliar territory in search of fulfilment, they

Caravan to Mecca

This illustration by Hariri, taken from a mid-13th-century Persian manuscript, depicts a company of travellers journeying to Mecca to make the hajj, *or pilgrimage.*

are deprived of their comfortable and habitual home life and subjected to trial and peril. In *Journey to the East*, the 20th-century writer Herman Hesse stated that every pilgrimage is part of the eternal striving of the human soul toward the East, the Home of Light. The inner compass of the spirit directs the way, but even with the longing for inner change, and courage to take the journey, the path can be lost if there is no guidance for the pilgrim. Direction can come either from a teacher or by following the ancient customs of established pilgrimage routes.

SACRED DANCE

Ekoi Tribe Dance Mask
*Masks conceal the identities of the performers and
confer on them the attributes and power of the deity,
spirit or animal that they are impersonating.*

When, having seen the Ark of the Covenant safely returned, David "danced before the Lord with all his might" (2 Samuel 6.14), he was responding to an instinct in all of us to dance for joy or thanksgiving. Through the ages, the ancient emotions that dance can stir within participants and spectators alike have been drawn upon during rituals of birth, renewal, love, death and war. Many dances are said to have been created by the gods, during the "time before time", so that to perform them is to re-create our sacred history.

There are many different kinds of sacred dance. Some, such as the dances of the Indian temple prostitutes, or *devadasis*, unfurl slowly using a vast vocabulary of hand gestures and facial expressions. Others are wild and uninhibited, such as the energy-summoning dances of the African Bushmen of the Kalahari. Among the many reasons for performance are to overcome evil spirits, to ensure good crops, to cure sickness, to meet

the ancestors, to attain power to defeat enemies, and to please the gods. In some sacred dances, the performer takes on the identity of the divine being; for this to be effective, the costume must express the magical quality of the deity. Masks are particularly significant because they contain the concentrated power of the god or spirit, concealing the earth-bound identity of the dancers and transforming them into new magical beings.

Dance and rhythmical music often induce changes in consciousness: trance and ecstatic states are common (see pages 146–7). One of the main dance dramas of Bali, in Indonesia, depicts the battle between the beneficent dragon-like figure of Barong and the evil witch Rangda. In this dance the followers of Barong, who have been bewitched, utter bloodthirsty cries as they attempt to push sharp knives into their naked breasts. The dancers have entered a state of trance and will eventually collapse to the ground, where they have to be revived with holy water.

Another dance that incorporated trance was that of the Mevlevi Order of Ottoman Sufis. The order was founded in the 13th century by the Persian Sufi poet Jalal ud-Din Rumi. Known as the "Whirling Dervishes", they sought to find ecstasy through spinning around in a movement that was intended to represent the order of the heavenly spheres. During the dance, one hand was held up in the air, open to receive the Divine Essence, and the other hand was held down toward the ground. In this way, the dancers were symbolically linked to both heaven and Earth.

Many sacred dances contain elements of terrestrial and spiritual renewal. Modern European maypole and morris dances have their roots in ancient round dances, which were performed to aid the Sun's journey through the heavens. In England, the rites remained joyous and uninhibited until they were condemned by the Puritans. In contrast, during the four-day Native American Sun Dance, held between late spring and early summer, participants would endure fasting, hours of dancing and self-torture in order to reaffirm their spiritual beliefs and assure the tribe's prosperity (see page 133).

In the late 19th century, Native American dance rituals were combined with Christian elements in the Shaker Church. Members of the sect practised a rolling exercise, which consisted of doubling the head and feet together and rolling over like a hoop. Somersaults were also performed by Hasidic Jews, although they were frowned upon. In their defence, practitioners would declare: "When a man is afflicted with pride, he must overturn himself." Hasidism is better known for its circular dance, in which each participant puts his hands on the shoulders of his neighbours in a symbol of unity.

Dance in all its forms seems to have always sought to heal and renew the soul, be it that of the individual participants or the great soul of the Earth itself.

Bull Leaping

The ancient Cretan custom of bull leaping may be a predecessor of the modern bullfight. Young dancers somersaulted over the bull – which symbolized divine potency – in a form of fertility ritual.

THE ACT OF PRAYER

Many of us associate prayer with stillness and quiet reflection in a place removed from the distraction and noise of everyday life. As a personal communication with or petition to the divine, prayer is understood primarily as involving the soul. However, in most spiritual traditions, prayer is believed to be at its most powerful when it combines reiterated physical action and speech.

Preparation for prayer often includes some form of ablution. Shinto worshippers wash their hands and rinse their mouths before ringing a bell or clapping to attract the gods' attention. Participants in North American traditions are brushed with burnt sweet-grass in a purification ceremony called "smudging".

The characteristic bodily attitudes of prayer – bowing, kneeling, prostration – are gestures of humble submission. On entering a church or approaching the altar, Roman Catholics genuflect, touching one knee to the ground to acknowledge the presence of the Body and Blood of Christ. They also make the sign of the Cross as a gesture of reverence. When visiting a temple, Hindu worshippers prostrate themselves in prayer outside the inner sanctuary, which only priests can enter.

Most organized prayers take one of five standard forms: supplication, adoration, praise, contrition or thanksgiving. While supplicating and contrite prayers are usually offered kneeling or bowing, gods may be praised or thanked standing with arms outstretched. The latter position invites the divine to enter into the heart. Hand positions are also important. In many cultures, people simply pray with their hands together or clasped. During Hindu and Buddhist rituals and dances, participants use *mudras*, or hand gestures, to convey hundreds of different concepts or principles.

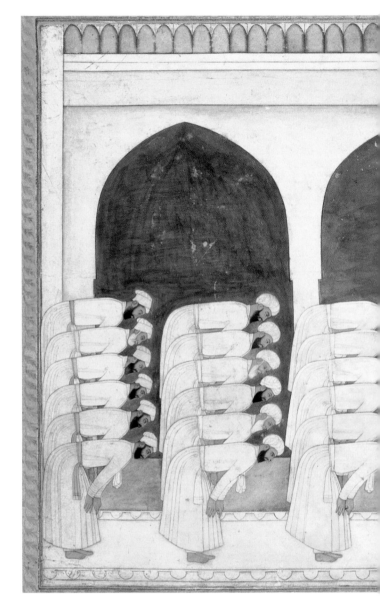

Offerings or sacrifices also play an important part in the prayer ritual, and are methods of honouring or appeasing the divine. In countries where food shortages are common, edible offerings can often be seen in temples and shrines. In cultures where money competes with the divine for worship, religions may suggest that a person should willingly give a percentage of his or her income to the church, mosque, synagogue or temple.

Ritual Hand Gestures

Mudras, *or hand gestures, are used in Hindu and Buddhist rituals and dances to convey key religious principles. A type of visual shorthand, this symbolic language uses hundreds of positions.*

Islamic Prayer

The ruku, *a bow with the legs and back kept straight, forms part of the set Islamic prayers, or* salat. *This 18th-century Mughal painting (left) depicts a prince leading the Friday prayers in a mosque.*

Although private prayer is recognized by every religion, public prayer as part of a congregation is thought by many traditions to be more uplifting. Both Jewish and Christian religious services combine song, readings and set prayers to create a specific, sometimes fervent atmosphere. Prayer is one of the Five Pillars of the Islamic faith, and on Friday afternoons congregational prayers at the mosque are obligatory. During the rest of the week, Muslims may perform the *salat* – the ritual of movements and words given in the Koran to be carried out five times per day – on their own. The first part of the prayer involves deliberately shutting out the distractions of the world. The splendour of Allah is acknowledged by standing to attention, raising the hands to shoulder level and proclaiming Allah as the most high. Then, as the hands are crossed over the heart, the prayer seeking shelter from Satan is chanted. Several prayers follow, alternating with bows, after which, aligning themselves toward the holy city of Mecca, the worshippers prostrate themselves at full length, touching the ground with hands, forehead, nose, knees and toes. Worship ends with a prayer for forgiveness, and the last action is the *salaam*, in which the head is turned from left to right to greet other worshippers and the watching angels.

The Koran openly states that such a rigid programme of prayer is meant, in part, to encourage believers to obey Allah unconditionally. Indeed, the word *islam* means the active recognition of, and submission to, the will of Allah. The physical actions of the *salat* help to channel worshippers' thoughts toward humility and thanksgiving, and to unite fellow believers.

THE WAY OF THE WARRIOR

To many of us, war is a great evil and has no place in a civilized society. However, warrior cultures were once widespread, and their influence can be found in the teaching and rituals of almost all of the world's religions. Great warriors, like saints, developed genuine fearlessness in the face of danger. Many have found that being able to confront fear directly overcomes physical and spiritual obstacles.

One of Hinduism's holiest books, the *Bhagavad Gita*, tells the story of Arjuna, a leading Pandava warrior, who was fighting for control of his country against the Kauravas. As the armies stood face to face, waiting for the final battle to start, Arjuna experienced a great doubt about the morality of what he was about to do and began to feel that it would be better to die himself than to kill his former friends, kinsmen and teachers. The god Krishna was acting as his charioteer. When Arjuna asked him what he should do, Krishna replied that he should fight. He explained that it was not possible for Arjuna, as an embodied soul, to stand back from the conflict. However, what binds us to the painful wheel of rebirth is emotional attachment in action, not action itself. The higher "self" is not involved in conflict, and it is possible to maintain a clear awareness of its changeless inner identity. Actions imprison us when we lose this identity with the inner "self". According to Krishna, if Arjuna did not act from personal attachment, he could

perform his role on the battlefield knowing that his innermost nature is untouched by all that happens.

Many religions teach that warfare is permissible, and even desirable, in defence of the faith. In the 11th, 12th and 13th centuries the Christian powers of Europe raised armies to retake the Holy Land from the Muslim Turks. Known as the Crusades, these military expeditions were infamous for their brutal treatment of the enemy. The unofficial Sixth Pillar of Islam is *jihad*, or striving, which is usually taken to mean holy war against the infidels; interestingly, *jihad* is also used to describe the personal battle to overcome one's inner passions and imperfections. In the face of Mughal hostility, the tenth Sikh Guru, Gobind Singh, instigated the Rahit, a code of discipline which, among its requirements, obliges all Sikhs to carry a sword or dagger.

In medieval Japan, contact between the samurai warrior class and Buddhist priests gave rise to questions about the ethics of killing, and new ideas developed about warriorship. Students of the martial arts learned to counter force without the use of aggression. Their aim was self-knowledge, leading to spiritual realization, and the weapons that had been used

Archangel Michael
As the Christian champion, Michael is usually portrayed wearing the breastplate of righteousness and the shield of faith. His sword is the word of God.

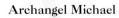

The Samurai

Members of the Japanese warrior caste were renowned for their military skills, stoicism and bravery.
Contact with Buddhist priests taught them to cultivate fearlessness toward death.

for slaughter were transformed into powerful spiritual tools. The Japanese longbow was a fearsome weapon, capable of piercing armour from immense distances. In Kyudo, the "Way of the Bow", the weapon became a means to cultivate inner balance of mind by combining meditation with mastery of the body. Because conscious control vanished in the meditative state, the archer was able to release the arrow without any notion of success or failure. However, his physical training ensured that the arrow would find its target with amazing accuracy.

Today, most of us acknowledge our wariness of aggressive physical energy, but the conquering hero who subdues evil remains an essential component of the human psyche. In transmuting such power into a spiritual quality, we recognize that the true enemy of our souls is false attachment to the lures of the material world.

SACRIFICE

Whatever spiritual path we may choose to pursue, it is never an easy option. In recognizing the limitations of earthly existence and accepting our inevitable mortality, we are required to sacrifice a superficial, worldly perspective for a greater reality. Renouncing self-centred actions or material indulgences for the benefit of others forms part of most religious traditions; some may also require the physical disciplines of periodic fasting or abstaining from sexual pleasures. In challenging the easy comforts of our everyday world, we seek to become more aware of the life of the soul.

The concept of sacrifice, whether on a literal or metaphorical level, has long been associated with religious traditions. Animate or inanimate objects have been offered to the gods for centuries in exchange for power, fertility, plentiful food supplies or victories in battle. Many faiths demand the renunciation by their followers of ordinary, habitual values.

This is perhaps most graphically exemplified in the Hebrew Bible's story of the *Akedah*, or the "binding of Isaac", which recounts God's command to Abraham, first of the three patriarchs of the Jewish people, to sacrifice his son Isaac on Mount Moriah. In preparing the sacrifice, Abraham places the honour and love of God above natural human laws; he is rewarded by divine intervention and the substitution of a ram for the

Aztec Sacrifice
This illustration from a 16th-century codex shows prisoners of war being sacrificed to the Aztec god of the Sun and war, Huitzilopochtli.

child. A prayer read during the Jewish festival of Rosh Ha-Shanah (see page 135) cites the *Akedah* as a supreme example of obedience to the divine will and a celebration of its merciful outcome: "Remember unto us, O Lord our God, the covenant and the loving-kindness and the oath which Thou swore unto Abraham our father on Mount Moriah; and consider the binding with which Abraham our father bound his son Isaac on the altar, how he suppressed his compassion in order to perform Thy will with a perfect heart."

In Christian belief the Son of God himself provides the sacrifice through which humankind's salvation is achieved. A worshipper wishing to follow Christ, according to the Gospel of St Matthew, must make a personal abdication of egotistical or worldly values: "If any man would come after me, let him deny himself and take up his cross and follow me. For whoever loses his life for my sake will find it."

Another instance of divine sacrifice occurs in Norse myth. The god Odin hung for nine days and nights on the World Tree, pierced with a spear, in order to gain his knowledge of the sacred runes used in divination – "myself given to myself". Odin's sacrifice, possibly of shamanic origin, was emulated by many of his cult who, anxious to share in his unique wisdom, underwent a ritual death by hanging and by spear.

Mystery of the Fall and Redemption of Man

Giovanni da Modena's 15th-century depiction of the Crucifixion shows Christ hanging from the Tree of Knowledge, the cause of Adam and Eve's expulsion from the Garden of Eden. In a complex inter-relation of symbols, the wood from the Tree of Knowledge is united with the Cross – the promise of Christian redemption.

Inca Sun God Sacrifice

Llamas were among the Inca's most prized sacrificial animals. When there was a new moon, herds were taken to the mountain-tops and offered to the Sun god, Inti.

SICKNESS AND HEALING

Although modern medicine defines health as "freedom from disease", the word originally meant "wholeness", and comes from the Anglo-Saxon root that also gave us the word "holy". Medicine, spirituality and magic were once viewed as limbs of the same discipline, but modern scientific medicine has become distanced from its archaic beginnings and, with its ground-breaking advances in surgery, victories over infectious disease and discoveries of wonder drugs, has put other types of healing in the shade. Recently, however, doctors have been accused of overlooking the causes of disease – both physical and spiritual – and so failing to promote the long-term health of their patients.

In ancient times, sickness was seen as a punishment from the gods; alternatively, witchcraft, demons and evil spirits were thought responsible for medical problems. The exorcism of evil spirits played an important role in the ministry of Christ, who was able to cure conditions ranging from blindness to insanity. "Madness" was an especially terrifying phenomenon – innocent sufferers were believed to be possessed by the devil and were often persecuted or killed. At other times the mentally ill were thought to have been touched by the gods and were treated as holy beings.

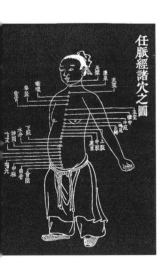

Chinese Medicine
Daoists believe that illness results from an imbalance of the female and male energies, known as yin *and* yang. *Some of the main centres of energy in the body are illustrated in this ancient Chinese medical diagram.*

Western medicine has its roots in the teachings of Hippocrates, a Greek physician who lived around 460–370 BCE. Doctors still invoke the ancient gods of Greece when they take the Hippocratic Oath, which opens with the lines: "I swear by Apollo the Healer and by Asklepios, by Hygeia and Panacea, and by all the gods and goddesses, making them my witness, that I will fulfil according to my power and judgment this oath."

At the time of Hippocrates, Hygeia and Asklepios represented two different approaches to healing. Hygeia's followers believed that health was the natural order of things and that the role of medicine was to help the body use its own innate powers of healing to cure itself. Many therapies in existence today, from both the Eastern and Western systems of healing, come under Hygeia's rule. Scientific medicine comes under the rule of Asklepios, who represented the belief that the physician's chief purpose was to treat the symptoms of disease caused by accidents or infections.

One of the chief roles of shamans and so-called "witch doctors" is to treat illness in the community. Chant, dance, prayer and powerful hallucinogenic drugs are used to provoke visions that reveal the causes of and cures for sickness. The two most common diagnoses are loss of soul, and possession. For the former, the shaman will attempt to find the patient's soul in the spirit world and persuade it to return to the body. When treating a person who is possessed, some shamans suck out the evil and vomit an actual object from their own mouths; others remove objects from the patient's body by psychic surgery. The shaman attempts to weaken the spirit of the perpetrator by magical means, thus safeguarding the strength of the patient.

Medicine Man

Modern drugs may seem unrelated to the natural world, but many are based on age-old herbal remedies. In this contemporary painting of a medicine man by Gayle Ray, the healer is surrounded by plants, which are the tools of his trade.

The healing power of belief, which may have been under-emphasized in Western medicine, is at the heart of many traditional schools, which believe that the body has the power to heal itself if the correct energies are accessed. In Chinese medicine, doctors rely on the technique of acupuncture – the insertion of needles along special lines, termed meridians (see page 48), on the body – to effect changes in the flow of energy to specific organs. An imbalance in the body's energy flows may be treated as soon as there is a general feeling of malaise, rather than waiting for more violent symptoms to develop. Chinese medicine is therefore well equipped to deal with illness in its earliest stages. In *The Yellow Emperor's Classic of Internal Medicine*, healing was compared to ruling a country; it was said that guiding those who were not yet rebellious was more effective than attempting to put down full-scale riots.

While Western medicine is spectacularly successful in treating the physical body and organic disease, more holistic healing methods may be better equipped to sustain our mental and spiritual welfare. Many healers do not see a conflict between their medicine and that of conventional doctors. They believe that their role is to address the fundamental imbalances that cause our bodies to fail – the deep spiritual roots of disease – while leaving scientific medicine to clear the more obvious, physical symptoms of illness that the body's own systems have failed to heal.

FEAR OF DEATH

The knowledge that we will die is the only certainty in the lives of all of us. In recent times, however, many societies have become distanced from death. Leaving the care of the elderly and infirm to experts, we desperately try to halt our own bodies from ageing, in a monumental exercise of denial. So the prospect of dying remains a source of primal terror, the dark underside that offsets the sensual indulgence of life.

The great psychiatrist Carl Jung believed that of all the body's failings, its most appalling betrayal was to die. The process of physical decay both fascinates and repels almost all cultures. Some form of *memento mori* ("reminder of death") features in many religions, emphasizing the transience of material existence compared to the life of the soul. In Hindu and Buddhist Tantra, meditation in the charnel ground, or graveyard, is viewed as a way of going beyond terror – adepts deliberately seek out horrifying situations in order to transcend revulsion and fear. Only in the charnel ground, among the imperfectly burned and decaying corpses, is it possible to accept fully the inevitable dissolution of the body and correspondingly to realize the illusory nature of egotistical identity.

The Grim Reaper
Death is commonly portrayed in the West as a scythe-bearing skeleton, who inexorably severs the thread of life from the dying and harvests their souls.

Representations of death often show its integral connections with life. The Hindu mother goddess Devi is both a loving provider and, as the fearsome Kali, the destroyer who gathers in the bodies of the dead. Kali is the frightful manifestation of death in the form of famine, smallpox and cholera. Her body is dark grey or blue and she wears a garland of snakes or skulls around her neck. She is accompanied by vultures, jackals and crows, who crunch on the bones of hideous corpses, and the walls of her temples drip with the blood of animal sacrifices.

Such vivid depictions of death challenge the reluctance of many cultures, especially modern secular ones, to acknowledge its presence and inevitability. Death is often viewed as a threatening stranger, as in the enduring Western image of the Grim Reaper, whose scythe shows his original association with the natural agricultural cycle of death, or decay, and renewal.

The judgment of the soul after death is integral to many religions, although the nature, severity and length of punishment for transgressions varies. Interpretations of Christianity made from the 5th century until relatively recently stressed that it was not possible to achieve

redemption from hell. Fear of death was made more intense by the belief that sins committed during life would be punished for eternity. Descriptions of hell from the Middle Ages, reflected with macabre fascination in the period's frescoes, told how intense claustrophobia, guilt, remorse, despair and extreme pain would be experienced in the searing heat or freezing cold of its realms. The torture was unending, and perceived in vividly physical terms: bodies would be sliced up, crushed or boiled, and reconstituted so that they could suffer again.

Eastern religions generally consider the realms of hell to be temporary stations in the cycle of death and rebirth. The Tibetan Lord of Death, Yama, judges the deeds of the newly deceased soul by looking at its reflection in the karmic mirror. If a person's actions are deemed to have been lacking or evil, his or her soul will be tortured until all guilt has been expiated. The Tibetan Book of the Dead includes Yama's description of bodily torments to be inflicted by the executioners: "They will put a rope around your neck, cut off your head, dig out your heart, pull out your guts, drink your blood, lick up your brain, eat your flesh and gnaw your bones; but you will not be able to die." However, he goes on to explain that the victim need not fear the Lord of Death if he or she can see the essential emptiness of both him- or herself and the deities. The soul's suffering can thus be seen as self-created, and can be removed by recognizing the true nature of the hallucination.

Yamantaka, Tibetan Conqueror of the Lord of Death
The terrifying Yamantaka is a bodhisattva *who has overcome his fear of death and is dedicated to helping those trapped in suffering. His bull's head and third eye link him to the Hindu god Shiva.*

CONFRONTING DEATH

Despite our understandable fear of the unknown, our need to recognize and accept the reality of death is an essential element of our development. From a spiritual perspective, death is an everyday, inevitable presence which gives sharper focus to our experience of life; by contrast, modern secular societies seek to minimize its significance. The fragility of the body was perceived by the Tibetan mystic Milarepa: "This thing we call 'corpse', which we dread so much, is living with us here and now," he observed, adding that avoiding the contemplation of death served only to increase human fear.

Spiritual philosophers have tried for centuries to help others accept death's inevitability. Plato described his work as "*phaidros melete thanatou*" – a joyous rehearsal and preparation for death which could inform the soul's understanding and appreciation of life. The Daoist master Zhuang Zhou described the folly of ignoring death through the example of a man disturbed by his own shadow. He tried to run from it, but the more he ran, the more the shadow kept up with him. As the shadow continued to follow him, he ran faster and faster until he dropped dead. He did not realize that if he stepped into the shade and sat down, his shadow would vanish.

By its very nature, the contemplation of death and its mystical separation of soul and body are usually expressed through metaphor and symbol. Meditational aids, such as the Buddhist *mandala* or the Shri Yantra

Christ on the Cross
Images of Christ's crucifixion, such as this 15th-century painting by the Flemish artist Rogier van der Weyden, remind Christians that the Son of God died to redeem their sins, offering them the possibility of resurrection after death.

pattern used in Hindu Tantra, celebrate the soul's union with the wider universe that enables the individual to transcend his or her physical death. Christian beliefs are rooted in the conviction that the death and resurrection of Christ offer hope of immortality to every penitent soul. Contemplation of Christ's Passion, through either stylized representations or the symbol of the crucifix, is an important aspect of the faith which brings the believer into direct confrontation with agonizing physical death. St Paul emphasized the integral relationship of life and death, observing: "I die daily, I crucify the flesh with its passions, I have no lasting city here." In the Orthodox Church, icons provide the focus for reflection and prayer. Remote and beautiful, in the formulaic Byzantine tradition, they offer the worshipper "windows on heaven" through which encounter with an unimaginable Godhead may be anticipated.

The rituals surrounding burial and mourning give spiritual guidance during an acute confrontation with death. Traditionally, family and friends prepare a corpse for cremation or burial and often undertake periods of ritual mourning, reflection and prayer. After a funeral, Jews observe seven days of mourning known as the *shivah* ("seven"). Family members receive visitors, but

Book of the Dead

In this judgment scene from a papyrus of the 14th century BCE, the heart, or conscience, of the scribe Hunefer is weighed against a symbol of justice and truth. The Devourer of the Dead squats by the scales ready to eat the heart if it weighs more than the feather.

leave the house only to attend the synagogue. The mourners are also required to refrain, as signs of grief, from bathing, having sexual relations or cutting their hair. The continuation of the deceased's soul is symbolized throughout the period by a burning candle.

Many spiritual traditions have sought to offer guidance to the dying and provide them with descriptions of the soul's passage after death. In ancient Egypt, extracts from the Book of the Dead – a compilation of sacred spells – were buried with rich members of society and included images of the deceased overcoming trials in the underworld. The Tibetan Book of the Dead describes death as a moment of piercing luminosity, or white light, before the soul begins its journey toward rebirth or liberation. Emphasis is placed on the importance of facing death courageously, allowing the soul to release itself calmly from the body.

For many centuries, confronting death was a way of facing a beginning as well as an end. The large body of European medieval literature on the subject, the *Ars Moriendi* or Art of Dying, sought to enable the Christian soul to overcome diabolic forces and reach paradise. By unflinching acceptance of the reality of death during life, the soul is able to blossom into its full maturity.

SURVIVAL OF THE SOUL

As we grow older and our bodies become weaker, we gradually withdraw from the physical world. For those who have had time to prepare for their death, the parting of the body and soul can be a smooth and peaceful transition. Others suffer an untimely or violent departure, sending shock waves through their families and communities. The rituals surrounding death may offer comfort to those left behind and aid the soul's journey in the afterlife.

One of the most widely held beliefs in the East is reincarnation, which in its simplest form is the conviction that at death the soul travels from the old body to a new one. Buddhism offers a more complex perspective, teaching that the soul is not an unchanging entity, but that it is the inherent energy of the subtlest levels of consciousness that takes new life. An analogy often used to explain reincarnation is the lighting of a new candle from one that has burned down. The force that drives rebirth is known as karma, the law that whatever action is carried out in a previous life will have a correspond-

Death and the Devil
The Mexican Day of the Dead is a celebration of life after death, realized in artifacts such as this painted wood carving of Death dancing with the Devil.

ing result in the next. Karma is thought to operate perpetually; the results of all actions will finally ripen when conditions are right. The Buddhist view of existence therefore takes into account deeds in past lives. As the Buddha himself observed: "What you are now is what you have been, what you will do is what you do now." Spiritual progress through correct action will eventually lead the spirit toward nirvana (see page 156) and release from the cycle of rebirth. At his own death, known as *parinirvana*, the Buddha is believed by worshippers to have achieved the perfection of complete and final extinction.

The Hindu religion also affirms that the soul, or *atman*, transfers smoothly from one body to another after death, when consciousness sleeps. Rather than praising past deeds, the Hindu funeral liturgy addresses the soul directly, encouraging its progress to another body as the pyre burns: "Depart, depart, by the ancient paths of our ancestors." Those unable to accept death, such as suicides or women who die in childbirth, become dangerous ghosts, or *preta*, who may frequent the

The Terracotta Army
An army of more than 6,000 life-size terracotta warriors was buried with the Chinese emperor Shi Huangdi (259–210 BCE) to protect him in the afterlife.

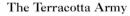

Footprint of the Buddha
In early Indian art the Buddha was never depicted as a man. After he had meditated through the many stages of his final extinction, his presence was symbolically represented by a pair of footprints.

outskirts of villages. Cremation is practised at most Hindu funerals, fire providing the means of transporting the *atman* to its next life. The body is readily discarded.

This is in stark contrast to the ancient Egyptian practice of making elaborate preparations for the afterlife, including the attempted halting of most bodily decay. The celebrated processes of mummification sought to provide a permanent body for the *ka*, one of the elements into which the soul was believed to divide after death. After mummification, rituals were carried out to re-animate the dead person's faculties so that the *ka* could see, hear, smell, breathe and eat; all the material sustenance needed for life was provided in the tomb. Another element of the soul was the *ba*, portrayed as a hawk with a human head. After death, the *ba* might attain the status of a spirit living with the gods. It could also reincarnate or suffer extinction. In ancient Egyptian belief, some souls either refused or were unable to enter the sphere of the dead; these were thought to be harmful to the living, and magical rites were practised to dispel them.

The beliefs that different cultures hold on survival after death profoundly influence their attitudes to the physical world. Few religions countenance a total extinction; most offer a wider perspective and purpose to individual existence through the enduring life of the soul.

The Burial of the Count de Orgaz
Universally regarded as El Greco's masterpiece, The Burial of the Count de Orgaz (1586–8) illustrates the myth that St Augustine and St Stephen descended from heaven to lay the count in his tomb – a reward for his generosity to the Church. The young boy to the left of the painting is El Greco's son, and the men in 16th-century dress are prominent members of Toledo society.

SEX AND GENDER

Many primal myths explain the creation of the cosmos in terms of the joining together of male and female. Conversely, some cultures see the creation as resulting from a breach or a split, so that what was one became two. In both cases, the fundamental act of creation centres around the complementary opposites of male and female. In Eastern cultures, sexual intercourse is often seen as a powerful symbol for the union of divine male and female principles, or as a way of becoming one with the divine. In the West, most religions promote a wholly spiritual union with the godhead. Male and female attributes have been associated with many pairs, such as darkness and light, Earth and sky, Sun and Moon, right and left or spirit and matter. Some consider that on their own, male and female are incomplete, and seek each other out to find wholeness and unity.

Krishna and the Maidens
The Hindu god Krishna is renowned for his ability to make women love him, convincing each of them that she is the sole object of his desire. The solicitous maidens in this painting of c.1710 are worshippers who desire to be thus united with the divine.

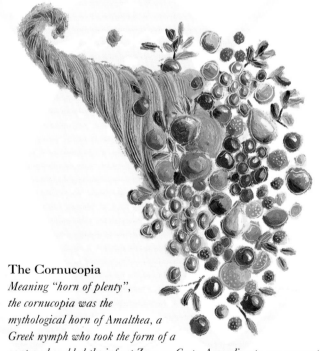

The Cornucopia
Meaning "horn of plenty", the cornucopia was the mythological horn of Amalthea, a Greek nymph who took the form of a goat and suckled the infant Zeus on Crete. According to one account, the god showed his gratitude by breaking off one of her horns and promising that it would be constantly filled with fruit, nectar and ambrosia. Being both phallic and hollow, the cornucopia symbolizes the productive union of male and female.

The Unicorn
This mythical beast is both a symbol of female virginity and, through its horn, of physical or spiritual penetration.

The Sun and the Moon
To alchemists, the Sun and the Moon were symbolic of the male (solar) and female (lunar) principles that had to be united in the fire of love in order to achieve perfection in the form of the philosopher's stone.

Hermaphrodites
Although all cultures recognize the physical and spiritual yearning for union with the opposite sex, most find beings that have both male and female characteristics disturbing. Nonetheless, myths relating that humankind was created by a divine hermaphrodite are widespread. This Roman statue shows a young hermaphrodite feeding the bird it is carrying.

IMMORTALITY

We have tended not to inflict the humiliation of decay and death on our gods and goddesses, preferring instead to imbue them with the qualities of perpetual youth and beauty that we so yearn for ourselves. Perhaps because of the continual renewal of the natural world, we have often used plants and animals as symbols of immortality. Some – like the crane – have been chosen for their physical attributes, others – such as the hallucinogenic plant the fly agaric – for their mood-altering properties. Mortals often acquired eternal life by eating food and drink normally

The Peach

Daoists believe that the peaches of eternal life are grown in the gardens of paradise.

reserved for the gods. Soma, for example, the "draught of immortality" drunk by the Vedic gods of ancient India, was also consumed by human participants in the Vedic sacrifice, who were given a brief glimpse of the ecstasy of immortality. In the modern age, some have opted to have their bodies frozen after death, hoping that regeneration will be possible in the future.

The Scarab

The dung beetle, or scarab, pushes a ball of dung comparable in form with the Sun. In ancient Egypt it was linked with the Sun's daily passage through the sky, becoming a symbol of renewal and regeneration. This scarab from the Papyrus of Anhai Book of the Dead dates from c.1250 BCE.

The Phoenix

In Classical myth, the phoenix was a bird with beautifully coloured feathers that lived in the desert. Every few hundred years it would burst into flames, only to be reborn from the fire's ashes three day later. It was a symbol of resurrection ad immortality in many different cultures.

The Hare in the Moon

In many parts of Asia, the hare is a symbol of longevity and fertility. It has close lunar associations, perhaps owing to the hare shape that is said to be visible on the surface of the Moon. In this 18th-century Chinese silk embroidery, a hare is portrayed mixing the elixir of immortality.

The Crane

In China, cranes (such as the one in this detail of a late 18th-century embroidered surcoat) were said to live for 1,000 years or more, and so symbolized immortality. They were believed to convey the souls of the dead to paradise.

FORMS OF THE SPIRIT

The soul or spirit is invisible to the human eye, but its unseen presence animates the natural world. Various descriptions of the spirit liken it to wind, smoke or vapour. Comparisons to a shadow or reflection express the view that the soul dwells in a similar, parallel universe, which is often a negative of our own world. Images of the soul are frequently connected with air and flight, and many cultures believe that, at death, the soul leaves the body in the shape of a bird or winged being. In medieval Christian iconography there are various symbols for the Holy Spirit, including a dove, the sails of a ship filled with the breath of God, and tongues of fire surrounding the Apostles or imbuing individuals with divine knowledge. Fire is also used as an image for the soul in Hindu mythology: flames licking around portraits of the gods and goddesses represent the powerful spirit energy of the deities.

The Falcon
Regarded as the king of birds in ancient Egypt, the falcon (seen here in a 3,000-year-old Egyptian sculpture) represented the flight of the soul after death. The sky-god Horus was either depicted as a man with the head of a falcon, or in complete bird form.

Bird–Woman Hybrids
In Greek mythology, sirens and harpies were bird–woman hybrids connected with violent death and the theft of souls. Sirens would bewitch sailors into driving their ships onto the rocks; the ghostly harpies stole human souls and carried them to the underworld. In southern Russia and the Ukraine, the souls of infants or drowned maidens were known as rusalka. *These spirit beings loved singing, but their voices were said to lure men to an untimely death.*

The Dove

Since the baptism of Jesus, when "the Spirit descended from heaven like a dove" (John 1.32), many have used the dove as a symbol of the breath of God (above).

The Ba

In ancient Egypt, a spirit-being known as a ba *was said to emerge from the body of a dead person. It was believed to have the head of a human and the body of a falcon.*

A Christian View of the Soul

In Simon Marmion's 15th-century work The Soul of St Bertin Carried up to God, *the naked, clean and pure-looking soul is being raised by two angels.*

Spirituality has been associated with the natural world since ancient times, when the power of the elements impacted directly upon human existence. Early hunters venerated the qualities of the animals they slew, and fertility rituals revered divinities to ensure the growth of essential crops. The physical forms of the

NATURE AND THE SOUL

Earth, as well as forests, rivers and other living features of its landscape, have long been regarded as sacred sites, expressing the presence of spirits or the creative authority of God. Modern lifestyles have distanced many of us from the natural world, and some believe that only tribal cultures retain a true spiritual appreciation of their environment.

THE SACRED EARTH

Many of us sense that the Earth we inhabit is in some way sacred. In religious traditions, it is a manifestation of a vital divine power – every crevice and undulation, every spring and river, is infused with spiritual meaning. We become most acutely aware of our own insignificance and transience in the perspective of unchanging mountains or the ceaseless breaking of waves on the seashore. Yet we may also find comfort through our affinity with the environment, and recognize that respect for the natural world is essential to our individual wellbeing.

Different landscapes carry their own spiritual identity, expressed through a particular topography. Many native peoples, such as the Maori of New Zealand, the Aboriginals of Australia and the inhabitants of Papua New Guinea, perceive in the Earth's relief indications of their ancestor spirits' presence and activities. Physical signs at sacred sites bear witness to the spirits' progress. These may include the marks of footprints or bodily impressions in the rocks, or boulders that represent ancient dung left by the spirits on their journeys.

Some cultures have fashioned their own spiritual symbols out of the Earth itself. The mysterious, man-made earthwork in Ohio created by Native American peoples more than 2,000 years ago is thought to be an effigy of the divinity known as Horned Serpent, which guarded sources of life, such as water, emerging from the Earth. Constructed in the form of a huge, uncoiling snake with an egg in its mouth, the effigy has obvious fertility associations. Archaeologists have also found evidence that fires were once lit on the summit, perhaps to give the impression of a vigilant and powerful presence.

Many early peoples believed that the physical surface of the Earth represented the body of a mother goddess

Moses on Mount Sinai

As the points on Earth that are closest to the heavens, mountains have traditionally been imbued with sacred significance. Mount Sinai is, according to the Hebrew Bible, the peak where Moses spoke to God and received tablets of stone inscribed with the Ten Commandments. Its precise identity is now unknown.

Mount Fuji

The snow-capped mountain in the background of this 19th-century painted fan is Mount Fuji. Japan's most sacred peak, it is believed to be a kami, *or spirit, and people climb it as an act of worship.*

(see page 16). Stones are still considered by some nomadic and hunting tribes to be protruding "bones", and rocky terrain is believed to harbour the vital spirit animating the universe. In Peterborough, Ontario, a weathered outcrop of crystalline limestone is covered with hundreds of diverse images, representing humans, animals, birds, solar boats, snakes, turtles and large solar figures who may portray gods. Although the meaning and function of these ancient carvings are unknown, crevices and hollows appear to link the rock to the underworld, and the echo of water from below may have been interpreted as spiritual voices. Gods and spirits were believed in many cultures to speak through cracks in the Earth's surface, often the sites of sacred oracles.

Rising toward the heavens, mountains have long been viewed as the home of the gods and served as their altars. They have also featured in most religions and systems of belief as places of vision and higher consciousness. Pilgrims seek to climb certain holy mountains as an act of worship in which the physical action symbolizes a spiritual ascent. Mount Fuji, in Japan, is held in the Shinto religion to be the physical embodiment of a *kami*, or divine spirit, and members of the Fujiko sect believe it to possess a soul. Several North American tribes, including the Lakota Sioux and the Cheyenne, visit Bear Butte – a sacred mountain ridge

on the plains of South Dakota – to pray and undertake vision quests (see page 136). The famous Lakota chief Crazy Horse is said to have experienced a vision of a bear spirit there in 1878, shortly before he defeated General Custer.

Mountains provide the setting for direct communication with God in both Jewish and Islamic religious traditions (see page 152). Suspended between earthly and heavenly realms, their slopes and summits offer a natural place for reflection and contemplation that enables us to feel closer to the spiritual world.

The Great Serpent Mound, Ohio

All over the world our ancestors made changes to the natural landscape, to emphasize or enhance its sacredness. One of the most striking examples is the Great Serpent Mound in Ohio, USA. This snake-shaped earthwork, 1,250 feet (380 m) in length, sprawls across the surrounding countryside.

SPIRITS OF NATURE

Maize

This silver head of corn, dating from the 15th- or 16th-century, reflects the reverence held by the Incas for their staple crop, maize.

For our ancestors, the recurring events of the natural world were divine in origin. They expressed the anger or beneficence of all-powerful gods, and lay far beyond human control. Early peoples venerated the power of nature spirits and gods, seeking to preserve and explain the seasonal cycles that sustained life. We may believe ourselves removed from the immediate impact of a bad harvest or a late spring, but most of us remain far from indifferent to the manifestations of nature, such as a beautiful sunset or snowfall, rolling mists or a violent thunderstorm. As we experience feelings of astonishment or alarm, we reaffirm the spiritual correspondences that continue to link us to the moods of the Earth.

Cultures that revere nature often perceive mutability as a natural feature of their environment. Some may recognize no gulf between the souls of humans and other creatures; a tribe's ancestors may be glimpsed and worshipped in animal form. The dual nature of a shaman enables his or her soul to manifest itself within an aspect or creature of the living world – the wind, foam on the ocean, a fish or a bird – in order to travel through water or air. Shamans of Amazonia are closely linked with the jaguar, whose form they assume with the aid of spells, talismans or hallucinogenic snuff; those of Siberia often take the form of reindeer or a loon (known as the diver in Britian). Many shamans can also incarnate the souls of distant ancestors, as well as nature spirits and gods.

Aspects of humans, plants and animals combine in nature spirits, who represent an amoral, untamed power beyond any human order. In Europe the Green Man, a spirit of lawless, burgeoning vegetation, still features in many seasonal festivals. Every January in Basle, Switzerland, he is brought down the Rhine on a raft in the guise of a Wild Man. Unleashed to dance through the streets, covered in leaves and brandishing a fir tree, he is the ambivalent spirit of the woodlands, symbolizing the natural impetus of rebirth. Pan, the ancient Greek god of flocks and herds, also embodies the wildness of the elemental world. The god's unseen presence, revealed by the eerie music of his pipes, was said to inspire sudden disorientation and fear; the word "panic" describes the effect on humans of such an encounter.

Many early nature gods had two distinct aspects: a shining summer form and a darker, underworld aspect of winter. Ishtar, the Akkadian goddess of love, war, fertility, childbirth and healing, was joined in sacred marriage with Tammuz, the god of growth and fertility. In an archetypal pattern of death and regeneration, Tammuz was killed with the harvest every year – the dying god was likened to a beautiful ear of corn, cut off in glorious ripeness by the reaper's scythe. Ishtar's bitter lamentation was reflected in the annual mourning of the whole community. The goddess followed her son-lover to the underworld, leaving the Earth in winter's grip: her miraculous return with Tammuz in the spring was celebrated as a divine miracle. A similar yearly cycle was enacted in the ritual marriage of the Anatolian goddess Cybele to her sacrificed son-lover Attis – the new grain was venerated each spring as the fruit of their union.

For peoples dependent on the harvest, their lives intimately linked to a seasonal pattern, the annual re-emergence of these deities was essential to survival.

Bacchus
The Roman god of both wine and ecstasy, Bacchus represented the wild side of nature. Known to the Greeks as Dionysus, he was the focus of a great mystic cult.

Shinto Charms
*These good-luck charms on a Shinto shrine are for the attention of local gods (*kami*), believed to govern the natural world.*

THE LIVING LANDSCAPE

Panorama of Varanasi
Many thousands of Hindus visit Varanasi each year to bathe in the Ganges. Many pilgrims come here to die, so that their ashes may be cast into this most sacred of Hindu rivers.

Certain places in the natural world still possess a strange, perhaps spiritual, charge, which we can sense almost immediately. These are often sites of ancient worship, where the *anima loci*, or "spirit of the place", was venerated as a local deity. Living features of the landscape – rivers and waterfalls, forests and sacred groves – were all believed to harbour spirits or gods who might bring power or protection to those who honoured them. In modern times, Shinto worshippers revere the *kami* who animate the material world, tying *gohei*, or white paper streamers, on trees to symbolize the *kami*'s enduring presence. The landscape remains the most sacred legacy of many native systems of belief, for whom affinity with the living world is part of their spiritual tradition.

Water is essential to all life and, especially when clear and running, a recurrent symbol of the soul. Consecrated water is frequently used in rituals, such as the Christian rite of baptism, to bring about healing, cleansing or spiritual awakening. Many of the most sacred Hindu sites lie along the shores of the Ganges. The river is believed to be the personification of the goddess Ganga and to carry the essence of *shakti,* or divine female energy, in its waters. Drinking and washing in the Ganges are important Hindu rituals, attracting thousands of pilgrims to the sacred sites of Varanasi, Allahabad and other holy centres. The river is a favoured location for scattering the ashes of cremated bodies, an action thought to allow the deceased's soul to bathe and purify itself in the sacred waters. From source to sea, the Ganges offers a channel of communication with the heavens: pilgrims at Gomukh, where the river rises high up in the Himalayas, believe that the winds rushing over the surrounding ice contain the voices of spirits; and prayer boats bearing flowers and candles are launched by worshippers in its lower reaches.

Often thought to link different levels of the cosmos, water also provides a demarcation between the realms of the living and the dead. The ancient Greeks, for whom much of the landscape revealed divine imprint, considered rivers such as the Acheron in northern

Nigerian Tree Spirits
Many cultures believe that gods or sprites dwell in trees. This shrine, a holy well dedicated to the goddess Oshun in Oshogoo, Nigeria, is guarded by spirit figures that have been sculpted out of a tree trunk.

Greece, which flows partly underground, to be connected to the underworld. Springs, associated with creativity, purification, fertility and regeneration, are thought in many cultures to be sacred openings to realms beneath the Earth. Sulla, a Celtic goddess of water and healing, was worshipped at the site of the thermal springs in present-day Bath in western England. She was identified with Minerva by the Romans, who constructed an elaborate temple complex in which suppliants requested the goddess's aid in healing, protection or vengeance.

Trees have also been invested with spiritual significance since earliest times. The image of the Tree of Life (see page 19) recurs in the creation myths of many cultures. In Angola, the Herero people believe the Omu-mboro-mbonga tree to be the place of origin of the first humans. Rituals surround the Life Tree of the Nepalese shamans, a solitary pine in which the shaman must endure a test of spiritual aptitude, and beneath which he or she may be interred after death. Hindus revere the banyan tree for its longevity and powers of regeneration, and sacred shrines are often located at the banyan's base. The sounds of wind blowing through a tree's leaves have long been interpreted as the voices of gods and spirits, contributing to the spiritual power of forests and groves.

FERTILITY

Fertility has always been viewed as one of life's greatest blessings, whether it relates to our individual capacity for conceiving children or to the Earth's ability to sustain plants and animals. Our dependency on nature's resources has expressed itself through spiritual practices from earliest times. Rituals evolved to ensure the fruitfulness of land and sea by honouring appropriate spirits and deities. Many of our spring religious festivals are still associated with the celebration of rebirth, often linked with the transcendence of death and return from the underworld. In acknowledging the spiritual cycle of death and regeneration, we are re-affirming our profound connections with the natural world.

Surviving folk customs and artefacts shed light on the ways in which early civilizations maintained the health and harmony of the land. Ancient stone carvings of the mother goddess, known as "Venus figures", are archetypal symbols of fertility, honouring a nurturing and protective Queen of Heaven and Earth. Her womb was seen as the vessel of creation from which all grains, fruits and vegetables flowed. A powerful fertility goddess featured in many early systems of belief. She appeared as Inanna in

The Green Man
A European fertility figure, the Green Man was said to control the rains.

Tlaloc
The Aztec rain deity Tlaloc was also a fertility god, as the maize harvest was dependent on his sending sufficient rain.

Sumer, Cybele in Anatolia, Gaia (see pages 16–17) and Demeter in Greece, the Magna Mater in Rome and Isis in ancient Egypt, where fertility depended upon the annual flooding of the revered Nile. The harvesting of crops heralded the barren season, when the goddess made her yearly descent into the realm of the dead, often in order to rescue her child or lover (or, through divine incest, both).

The sacred marriage of the goddess and her consort was re-created in fertility rites around the world. A high priestess and the reigning Sumerian king, for example, would enact the divine congress at the autumn equinox. Across Europe the May Queen was symbolically married to the Green Man in a ceremony to promote the Earth's renewal. To ensure fertility in Ireland, the king was obliged to marry a white mare, who represented the deity of the land. This Celtic rite strongly resembles the Vedic horse sacrifice in India, when a horse was smothered to death before the queen lay with it.

One of the most widespread fertility customs was a form of ritual orgy. This usually took place in the spring, when the Earth could be made fruitful by a couple having intercourse in a ploughed furrow. In ancient hunting cultures, animals were encouraged to mate by men and women who imitated their rutting. Ritual copulation could also be used for more directly personal gain. At Cerne Abbas in southern England, a naked male figure cut into the chalk was seen as a potent source of fertility; and traditionally, childless couples sought to conceive by copulating on the giant, preferably on his sexual organs.

Prayers for fertility are probably one of the oldest of all personal petitions to the gods. Many shamanic cultures believe that there is a limited number of souls in the world. If a woman is unable to conceive, she may ask the shaman to track down a soul for her child, as her infertility could be caused by a lack of availability.

The main crop of an agricultural community, whether it was rice, corn or maize, was frequently venerated as a deity, upon whose favour survival itself depended. Blood sacrifices were often made to these gods, as blood was perceived by many cultures to be a kind of soul substance, capable of generating new life. The Mayan peoples of Central America, whose staple food was maize, worshipped the crop as a god, in whose honour the nobles of the kingdom let blood from their tongues, earlobes and genitals. Rainfall, essential for the maize's growth, was believed by the Mayans to be in the care of the terrible god Chacmool, who was also desirous of freshly spilled blood.

Through the ages, humans have performed fertility rites to ensure a good harvest, to please the animal spirits, to bear a child, or simply to celebrate the abundance of nature. Many of us today, however, are cocooned from the extremes of winter and summer, able to buy an array of fresh fruit and vegetables all year round – but out of touch with the Earth's natural cycle.

Ceres

Ceres is the Roman version of the Greek goddess Demeter, who was believed to protect the crops and the bounty of the soil. As the goddess of corn, Ceres has given us the word "cereal".

LINES OF FORCE

In recent decades humankind has embarked upon an unprecedented exercise to alter the face of the Earth. We have felled forests, drained marshes, diverted rivers and constructed a massive network of roads to link our sprawling towns and cities. But beneath these scars, the Earth's own energy still flows along its ancient, deep and mysterious courses.

At those places where the Earth's spiritual pulse can be felt most acutely, our ancestors often built enigmatic structures or carved vast images. Some of the most mysterious markings on the planet are to be found on the Nazca plain in Peru. These are immense drawings of geometric figures, spirals, monkeys, whales, condors, flowers and fantastic creatures, some of them more than 1,000 feet (300 metres) long. The artists who perfected these beautiful figures knew that the only way for them to be seen was from the sky. It has been variously suggested that the images were meant to be viewed by the gods, by souls ascending after death, or by shamans in visions obtained during soul "flights".

The belief held by many cultures that there are paths of energy running through the landscape is the basis of the science of geomancy, which aims to harmonize human dwellings and activities with the physical and spiritual world. The ancient Chinese geomantic system known as *feng shui*, literally "wind and water", recognizes and interprets the invisible energy lines, known as "dragon veins", that reach down from the sky into the

Nazca Lines
These markings on the Nazca plain outline the body of an enormous bird with a snake-like neck (its head has been defaced). The complete creature could only have been visible from the air.

mountains and through the ground. These energy lines fall into one of two categories: the positive, life-enhancing *chi* and the negative, perilous *sha*. *Feng shui* teaches that if a dwelling is properly placed, it will be in harmony with the land's energy, rather than blocking it. The perfect building site has high mountains behind, smaller protective hills at the sides and flowing water at the front, but an imperfect site can be altered to change the energy. It is said that a geomancer can improve the *chi* of a landscape by placing temples or pagodas on the summits of mountains, in order to harmonize the magic forces of heaven and Earth. Some places, usually wild, mountainous regions, are too powerful to be inhabited; others, usually flat and featureless landscapes, are too sleepy and need to be woken up. It is said that a network of stone walls in a valley will domesticate the wild energy that tumbles from the mountains, while church spires and windmills will enliven a sleepy plain.

Belief in energy lines thrives still in the Western world. In 1922, businessman Alfred Watkins claimed to have "rediscovered" a system that connected all the sacred centres in England with what he termed "ley lines". He came to his conclusions a couple of years earlier, when, riding through Herefordshire one evening, he had a vision that all the landscape's tumuli, megaliths

St Michael Ley Line
The church of St Michael de Rupe in Brentnor, Devon, is built on a ley line linking St Michael's Mount in Cornwall to the abbey at Bury St Edmunds in Suffolk.

and stone circles were connected by shining paths – golden veins standing out amid the green and brown of the land. Watkins believed that the paths were Neolithic trading routes, or "old straight tracks", which linked many pagan (later, Christian) sacred sites through a practical network of physical landmarks. Watkins' theories are controversial, but aerial photography has revealed evidence of mysterious lines in the landscape, often appearing to link the most ancient places of sanctity. A ley line in southern England with Salisbury Cathedral at its centre also connects with Stonehenge and other Neolithic sites. The longest line in Britain links a series of churches dedicated to St Michael, the dragon slayer. A dragon's energy was believed to be fixed to the spot where it was killed, and the churches may be sited on pre-Christian shrines to the dragon's primordial power.

One of the most accepted ways of following a ley line or revealing the Earth's hidden energy is by dowsing. The dowser uses a forked stick, which is drawn irresistibly downward when it crosses underground water.

Around the world there is a growing body of evidence that our ancestors were able to access the Earth's hidden energy. Many today believe that by recognizing this energy, and learning to live in harmony with it, much of the daily stress we encounter will simply disappear.

SPIRIT OF THE HUNTERS

Before our ancestors practised basic crop-growing and animal husbandry, they survived through hunting and gathering. Not only were animals an essential source of food, but their skins could be used to make clothing and their bones implements. The importance of the hunt is revealed in some of the oldest-known cave paintings, which depict animals such as bison, musk ox, reindeer, woolly rhinoceros and mammoth. These may have been painted as a magic spell to draw the animals to the hunters, or after a successful hunt to ensure that the animals' spirits returned to the Earth. Alternatively, they may have been a celebration of the Earth's generosity.

In the cave of Les Trois Frères in France is a group of some 280 paintings and engravings of humans and animals, which date from the Late Paleolithic Era (*c.*40,000–*c.*10,000 BCE). The most remarkable figure is painted high on the wall, peering down at the visitors. His penetrating, owl-like eyes are set in a body that is half-man and half-beast, with deer's antlers and ears, and human legs, feet and hindquarters. His stance suggests that he is dancing. Nicknamed "the sorcerer", the figure has been identified as a shamanistic Master of Animals, strengthening the argument that shamanism is the world's oldest religion.

In hunting societies, the shaman ensured that an animal was killed according to the correct ritual. People believed that animals gave up their bodies willingly to the hunter, as long as they and their spirit keepers were properly respected. If the correct ritual was observed, the animal's soul would return in a new body the following season. Among the Inuit in Alaska, it was believed that the Old Woman of the Seals provided fish, seals, walruses and whales to the people. If she was displeased,

Diana the Huntress
This Roman fresco depicts the hunter-goddess Diana (the Greek Artemis), who fiercely protected the young of the animals she killed.

Cernunnos

Cernunnos, whose name meant "The Horned One", was the Celtic Master of Animals – a god of nature, fertility and plenty with strong links to the Otherworld. The antlered god was often portrayed with animals, especially stags and snakes, and wearing a torc (a twisted metal necklace) as a symbol of his divinity. Cernunnos is believed to be the forerunner of the Wild Huntsman of European mythology.

however, she withheld her bounty, and food became scarce. The shaman would then have to visit the Old Woman and try to effect a reconciliation. If he or she was successful, the animals returned.

All hunting depended on the acknowledgment of a spiritual affinity between the hunter and the hunted. Tribes heavily dependent on animals venerated certain species as their ancestors, and were prohibited from eating these totem animals. Many ancient gods were worshipped in animal form, and devotees sought to gain divine powers through symbolic costumes and rituals. For example, a bear was the cult animal of the Greek goddess of the chase, Artemis, and in their worship of her young Athenian girls would dance in bear-masks. Appropriately, Artemis was seen as the protectress of wild animals as well as the goddess of the hunt.

To the Celts, the hunt had associations with the Otherworld, and ancient myths told of enchanted animals luring hunters to the world of the dead. These myths resurfaced across Europe in tales of the Wild Huntsman, who made a bargain with the devil and was doomed to hunt forever. The Gabriel Hounds, whose appearance foretells death in a community, were another manifestation. In the Middle Ages the stag became a symbol of the wandering pagan soul, lost in the forests of life and hunted by the holy servants of Christ.

As hunting for food has become less necessary, the hunter has been increasingly portrayed as a bloodthirsty opponent of the spirit. In an age of animal rights it is hard to appreciate the mysterious connection between the human and animal worlds, the hunter and the hunted, that once conferred spiritual significance on the chase.

DREAMTIME

Ayers Rock, Australia
*A sandstone outcrop, Ayers Rock (Uluru), is one of the Aboriginals'
most sacred sites. It is said to have risen from the flat ground during
the Dreamtime, as a monument to an epic battle between two tribes
of the Sky Heroes.*

When European settlers first entered the Australian
heartlands, they found a featureless landscape as desolate as the surface of the Moon. The Aboriginals who
inhabited this "hell on Earth" were viewed by the
newcomers as a "Stone-Age race", unable to
adapt to modern life. As knowledge of their
beliefs and customs has grown, however, the
Aboriginals are increasingly seen as a people
who have retained a rare and important
respect for the land, founded upon spiritual
belief. Today, their relationship with the
planet is studied by many who wish to
connect with the Earth's primordial forces.

The Aboriginals believe that the world was
initially unformed and featureless.
Then, in the deep mythic past,
during a time known as the

Aboriginal Shield
*This pubic shield, made from shell, is
inscribed with mythological figures.*

Dreaming, Dreamtime or Creation period, the Sky
Heroes appeared and lived on the Earth. These ancestors journeyed across the world, forming and naming
every mountain, plain, river, tree, insect and animal.
They also created the souls of every individual. The Sky
Heroes left numinous traces of their presence in the
landscape, which are constant reminders of the world's
sacredness. One of the most famous sites in Australia is
Ayers Rock, or Uluru as the tribal people know it. This
vast landmark is a monument to an epic battle between
two tribes of Sky Heroes, the Liru (Poisonous Snake
People) and the Kunia (Carpet Snake People). Every
shape, mark, hollow and boulder was formed as a result
of this battle: three rock holes show where Ungata, the
leader of the Kunia people, died; the water that flows
down the rock face is Ungata's blood; the severed nose of
the Liru warrior Kulikitjeri has metamorphosed into a
boulder; three vertical gashes on the eastern rock face
record the wounds inflicted on Kulikitjeri by Liru;
a cave complex on the rock is the womb and
vulva of Bulari Minma, who gave birth there
at the height of the battle; her child lies at the
entrance as a large stone.

There are many Sky Heroes, but the
most important is the Rainbow Serpent –
often depicted swallowing people and then
regurgitating them in a transformed state as
features in the landscape. The theme of
swallowing and regurgitation is symbolic of
the transition from one state to another and is
often built into rituals to aid the
transportation of the initiate to a
higher spiritual level. The holy men

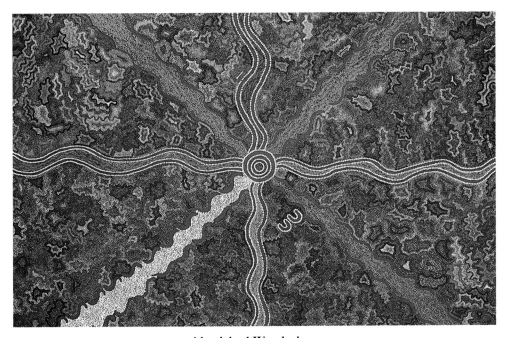

Aboriginal Wanderings

Modern depictions of episodes from the Dreaming are, like the landscape itself, difficult to interpret.
They may show the routes taken by the ancestors and sites that are imbued with their power.

of the Aboriginals used to undergo terrifying and painful initiation ceremonies, in which their bodies were scarred and pierced by pieces of rock crystal. They risked death at the hands of the spirits and went on long periods of meditation in the outback. Empowered by such spiritual practices, they were able to serve as a contact between their people and the spirit realm.

All Aboriginals, however, can connect with the spirits by undertaking the Dream Journey. The journey's origins may lie in migratory hunting practices, but on a ritual level it is a way of renewing self-contact, the identity of the land being inseparable from personal identity. By visiting sacred places, known as hotspots, travellers repeat the world-creating events of the original Dreaming. The hotspots, often waterholes, mark the places where the Rainbow Serpent re-entered the Earth.

The Dreaming can also be recalled through rituals, performed on any piece of land. During these ceremonies, the men chant in a circle to the accompaniment of eerie rhythmic music. The chants invoke the names and feats of the Sky Heroes, and continue until the spiritual energy is strong. Dancers then appear and re-enact the events of the Dreaming. At this point, all the participants in the ritual are said to have become Sky Heroes and, in that joyous and ecstatic state, are able to take part in the original mythic creation of the world.

In recent years environmental pressures have forced humankind to reassess its treatment of the planet. As we search for a sane and sustainable way of using resources, the ancient knowledge of the Aboriginals – that we are custodians of the Earth – is gaining recognition as a spiritually informed approach from which we can all learn.

AIR

Air is the most intangible of the elements; it is insubstantial and unseen, yet necessary to animate all living things. The significance of air was partially recognized by some of the earliest cultures, who chose suffocation as the method of sacrifice in their religious ceremonies. Air is the natural medium of the intangible soul, filling the expanse that divides the heavens from the Earth below. Those gods and goddesses who are believed to inhabit the air are generally of more recent origin than terrestrial deities. They successfully usurped their predecessors by offering those who worshipped them freedom from the physical limitations of worldly existence. The complex symbolism that surrounds air tends to focus on related phenomena that are easier to envisage, such as the sky, wind, flight and breath. Therefore, the Hebrew word *ruah* means both wind and, in the Old Testament, the breath of God.

Buddhist Prayer Flags
Prayers from these flags are carried in the wind around this Buddhist stupa in the Katmandu Valley, Nepal.

The Winged Creatures of Ezekiel
This Jewish book illustration (left), dating from 1348, shows four winged creatures – a man, a lion, an ox and an eagle. Similar creatures were described by Ezekiel in the Hebrew Bible and were possibly manifestations of the spirit of God. They were later adopted as symbols of the Christian Evangelists (see page 159).

Isis
The powerful ancient Egyptian goddess Isis is shown here with the sun disk, cow horns and throne of Egypt on her head (right). In other manifestations she appears as a kite or a winged goddess fanning the breath of life with her wings.

The Thunderbird

This Pawnee Ghost Dance drum of c.1890 is painted with an image of the Thunderbird. A Native American spirit in the form of a giant eagle, the Thunderbird embodies powerful weather forces, such as rain, thunder and wind.

The Oracle of Zeus

Situated at Dodona in the northwest of Greece, the Oracle of Zeus was an important source of divine knowledge. The answers to questions about the future were believed to be conveyed by the sound of the wind rustling leaves and stirring metallic objects hung in the sacred oak tree. A bough from the tree was incorporated into the Argo, *the ship that carried Jason and his companions on their quest for the Golden Fleece.*

Prana

Many Eastern philosophies believe that the vital force that energizes both human beings and the cosmos is carried in the air, entering our bodies when we breathe. This fundamental energy, symbolized by the central glyph above, is called prana *in India,* chi *in China and* ki *in Japan.*

FIRE

Since our earliest ancestors first learned how to make fire, the flame has been worshipped as the essence of divinity and the source of light. Fire is a complex symbol with many conflicting aspects; it can be creative or destructive, divine or demonic, providing gentle heat or devouring everything in its path. Its flames can represent the heat of passion, the force of inspiration or the brilliance of divine light. As a source of warmth and illumination, fire has often been seen as a symbol of the soul. Traditionally, festivals of light are held during winter to encourage the return of the Sun's life-giving power. Common to many cultures is the belief that, at the end of a cosmic era, fire will purge the world, and restore it to its original pristine state.

A Ship Funeral
In Scandinavia, the ship was a symbol of the fertility deities known as the Vanir. Important members of society, such as Viking chiefs, were often cremated in their longships, surrounded by ritual objects, weapons, personal possessions, horses, cattle, dogs and birds.

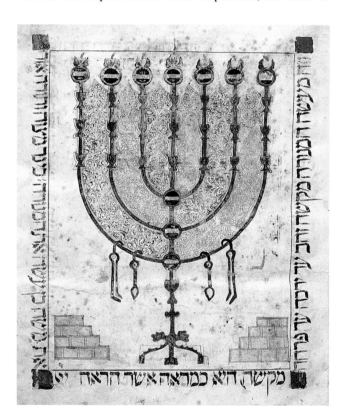

The Menorah
The menorah, a seven-branched candelabrum used in the first and second Jewish Temples, is an ancient symbol of spiritual light. It is one of the most sacred and powerful emblems of Judaism.

Agni

The Hindu god of fire, Agni (above), is both an invincible warrior and a domestic presence in the hearth of every home. He devours the corpses in the cremation ground and carries offerings to the other gods, often riding the sacrificial ram.

The Paschal Candle

The candle is a Christian symbol of Jesus as the "Light of the World" (John 8.12). Orthodox Christians announce Easter by the priest lighting a single flame – the Paschal Candle (left) – in a dark church, and announcing "Christ is risen!"

Ra-Harakhty

In most periods, the fiery Sun god was the principal deity of Egypt. This stela of c.1000 BCE portrays a woman worshipping the falcon-headed Ra-Harakhty – a manifestation of the rising Sun – who radiates beneficial rays toward her.

EARTH

In former times, traditional societies did not see the Earth as an inanimate body of rock and clay, but as a living being with a soul. The whole world was regarded as sacred: the creative powers of the universe were believed to direct the recurring cycles of the seasons, and spiritual forces were said to have shaped the very forms of the Earth's crust. Certain features of the landscape, such as rocks, mountains, caves, cliffs, islands and springs, were recognized as being the dwelling places of local deities and were often decorated with carvings or paintings. Trees that grew in these areas were regarded as particularly sacred, because their roots dug into the depths of the Earth and their branches reached up into the heavens, forming a link between the physical and spiritual worlds. Standing stones, shrines and temples were erected on propitious sites, and were kept sacred by priests and priestesses who communicated with and honoured the Earth spirit. Later religions either took over the sites for their own spiritual purposes or renounced them as the homes of demons.

Standing Stones
Megaliths, or standing stones, are massive, undressed blocks of stone, which were laboriously quarried and erected across the landscape of northwest Europe during the period 3200–1500 BCE. Although their purpose is obscure, they could have associations with astronomy or have been used during sacred rituals, such as fertility rites to the Mother Goddess.

Cave Temples
Rock-cut caves express the desire for unity between the human spirit and the ancient body of the Earth. These cave temples were created by Buddhists in Maharashtra, India.

Diamonds
Because of their immense hardness, diamonds are associated with eternity.

Jade
A semiprecious stone, jade is revered by the Chinese, who regard it as a manifestation of the Jade Emperor, the head of the Daoist pantheon.

Taurus
In astrology, the bull is the strongest and most fertile of the three Earth signs. This Persian image is from the 17th-century Wonders of the World.

Gold
A precious and dense element, gold is used by cultures throughout the world to symbolize the rays of the Sun.

Rubies
These blood-red gemstones have been regarded as symbols of royalty, power and passion.

Silver
Because its colour is reminiscent of the cool light of the Moon, silver has lunar, feminine associations and is a symbol of virginity.

Petroglyphs
Prehistoric drawings or carvings on rock – such as this mythical being found near Peterborough, Ontario – may mark the sites of physical or spiritual events. They may also be invocations to the gods to ensure the prosperity of the tribe.

WATER

Through the ages, pools, lakes, sacred wells and springs have been invested with magical properties. Many were believed to be the dwelling places of gods or supernatural beings, and so were seen as rich sources of both physical healing and spiritual transformation. Rivers provided the communication routes of ancient societies and also formed boundaries between spiritual realms: many tales of the underworld describe a land bordered by rivers. A universal symbol for the soul, water assumes many forms and has very different moods and qualities. It is as powerful as the ocean tides, as gentle as rain, as hard as ice and as soft as snow. Even as life on Earth cannot long endure without water, so the body cannot survive without the soul. Cleansing or baptism in steam or in running water often symbolizes a return to purity, washing away the old life to be born anew.

The Lotus Flower

The sacred lotus, a type of water lily, grows upward from the mud at the bottom of a pond and reveals a beautiful flower when it reaches the water's surface. It is a powerful symbol for the flowering of the enlightened soul.

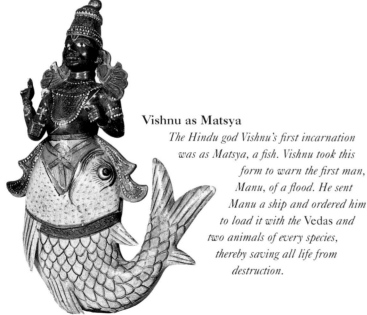

Vishnu as Matsya

The Hindu god Vishnu's first incarnation was as Matsya, a fish. Vishnu took this form to warn the first man, Manu, of a flood. He sent Manu a ship and ordered him to load it with the Vedas *and two animals of every species, thereby saving all life from destruction.*

The Fall of Babylon

The Mesopotamian city of Babylon became a metaphor for the excesses of human ambition. Christian commentaries on the biblical Apocalypse, such as this 10th-century Liebana Beatus *from Guadeloupe, gleefully depicted the city's sins being washed clean.*

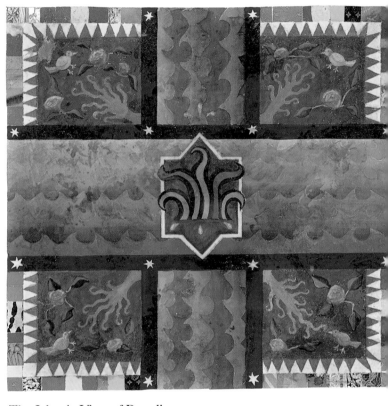

The Islamic View of Paradise

Water plays an important role in descriptions of heaven, which often include a landscape irrigated by fountains of youth and streams of milk and honey. The Islamic vision of paradise consists of a series of luxurious gardens with four rivers radiating from the centre.

The Baptism of Christ

The first three Gospels of the New Testament describe how Jesus was baptized in the River Jordan by his cousin, John. Today, baptism is one of the Christian sacraments: a person's sins are ritually washed away, before he or she is believed to receive the Holy Spirit.

SACRED ANIMALS

Animals have been regarded as sacred symbols since earliest times. Hunting communities invested their quarry with spiritual significance, and the hunts themselves were sometimes viewed as acts of veneration to the gods. Deities of ancient religious traditions were often represented in animal form: the association of the Mother Goddess with lions, for example, has probably existed since Paleolithic times. Some cultures discovered animal forms in the skies: constellations in the shape of the Ram, Bull, Crab, Lion, Scorpion and Fish were first percieved by the Babylonians, and later integrated into the Western Zodiac. Animals also played an important physical role in religious ceremonies. The movements of birds and animals were studied to divine the future, and the favour of the gods was sought through regular offerings of blood from sacrificial beasts.

Today many native cultures trace their ancestral roots back to sacred animals – living totems, which assume protective roles over their descendants. Some tribal peoples believe that they possess an animal, as well as a human, soul, and teach that inner integration and wholeness are dependent on harnessing and accepting the power and energy of the animal component.

Bastet
Cats were worshipped in ancient Egypt as manifestations of the cat-headed goddess Bastet. Often depicted with kittens, this benign deity was associated with motherhood, sex and fertility. Mummified cats were frequently buried close to the goddess's shrines.

A Haida Drum Cover
To the Haida people of British Columbia, the bear is a powerful spirit helper. This shamanic drum, used by the shaman to summon the spirits, is decorated with a bear.

Imaginary Beasts

This image from a medieval bestiary shows Christ in Majesty, surrounded by stylized angels. He sits in splendour above four beasts, whose features have been drawn from various animals.

Bees

The communal organization of bees, collecting pollen, building and cleaning combs, producing honey to feed the young, and guarding the hive, made them symbols of diligence and courage.

Birds

Because flight has long been associated with the ascent of the soul, gods and goddesses are often portrayed in bird form. This painted wood carving from northwestern New Ireland, Melanesia, is of a mythical sky being.

The Chinese Dragon

In China, the dragon is thought to bring good luck. It has five major manifestations, each of which influences important aspects of life. The Imperial Dragon (pictured above in embroidered silk) symbolizes both the rain and the rising Sun. In its other forms the dragon's duties include guarding the heavens and controlling the sea.

The Tortoise

In many cultures, the tortoise (as in this pre-dynastic Egyptian carving) symbolizes the cosmos. Its body represents the Earth, protected by the shells of heaven and hell.

Snakes

The Rainbow Serpent is considered the most important ancestor of the Australian Aboriginals. Billy Stockman's Snake Dreaming *shows the snake's progress across the Earth during the Dreaming.*

The Sacred Cow

This batik painting from Kashmir in India portrays a white cow – considered sacred by Hindus – decorated for a festival.

Garuda

Half-man and half-bird, Garuda is the vehicle of the Hindu god Vishnu. He is depicted in this 18th-century painting carrying his master and Vishnu's consort Lakshmi, the popular goddess of prosperity and good fortune.

Mithras and the Bull

The Persian god Mithras became the centre of a Mystery Cult during the Roman Empire. Mithras was usually portrayed slaying a great bull, which symbolized his animal nature. Initiates into the cult of Mithraism were baptized in the blood of a bull.

Most of our spiritual traditions acknowledge the existence of realms beyond the material. Some beliefs consider these to be accessible only after death, when the soul is liberated from the constraints of a physical body. Others, especially those of shamanic cultures,

THE SPIRIT WORLD

regard voyages between realms as possible in life – often achieved in dreams or trance states, and assisted by spirit helpers. The proximity of spiritual and physical worlds, especially at certain times of the year, has an ambiguous aspect in many faiths. The spirit world may be represented as a source of sacred knowledge, comfort or healing wisdom. However, travel to another realm is seen as a dangerous business, which, whether undertaken in life or after death, requires informed spiritual preparation.

SOUL REALMS

In our spiritual beliefs, many of us are drawn to the idea of existence beyond the material world. Our conception of such realms, in which the soul escapes the limitations of a physical body, may be shaped by religious tradition or by our own imaginings and experiences. The idea of the soul wandering in dreams or trance, for example, is a common conviction among tribal peoples and still retains a hold on the Western psyche. Near-death experiences, recounted by those brought back from the brink of physical extinction, offer us a further, often comforting, perspective on the soul's potential for entering into another world.

The human realm is generally placed in the middle layer of the spiritual universe, with the heavens above and an underworld, usually associated with the souls of the dead, below. The World Tree (see page 19) often links the different cosmological tiers and in some cultures offers the possibility of moving between them. Water also provides a traditional demarcation of different realms, and crossing over water is a complex symbol, associated with forms of spiritual rebirth. In ancient Greek mythology, souls were brought across the River Styx by Charon the boatman to the province of the dead, known by the name of its ruler, Hades. Modern Hindu traditions venerate the sites of unusual natural phenomena in the landscape, which are known as

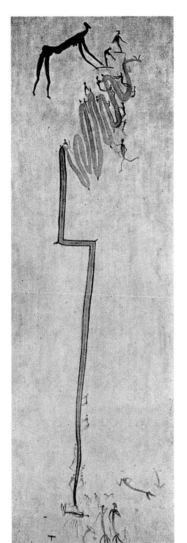

The Spirit in the Sky
In this southern African rock painting, a tree is shown growing from the body of a woman sacrificed to the spirit who dwells in the sky.

tirthas (meaning "fords" or "crossings"). These sacred sites are often literally fords, but they may also occur in mountain crevices or rivers, or on plains. *Tirthas* represent places where a divine presence enables those pure in spirit to move temporarily beyond the physical world to a transcendent, spiritual realm.

The Buddhist Wheel of Life can be interpreted either as a map showing states of mind, or as a literal guide to other worlds – all potential places of rebirth. The Wheel's lower spokes depict the realms of animals, hungry ghosts, and several regions of hell, ranging from the frozen worlds of permanent snow and ice to one resembling a furnace. Illusion is often set at tormenting variance with reality in these nether hells. The apparently beautiful countryside of the hell known as the "Plain of Knives", for example, is agonizing for its inhabitants to walk upon. However, in contrast to other religions' eternal hells, the tortured souls will eventually be released through the Buddha's compassion, and will be reborn elsewhere. Even the heavenly realm of joy and flowers, set at the top of the Wheel of Life, is subject to mutability, despite its pleasures and

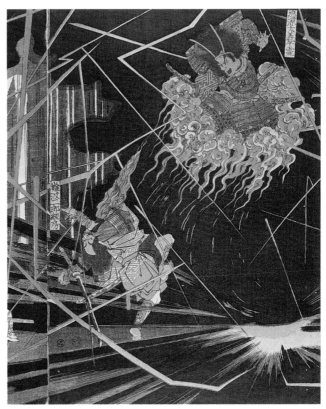

The Buddhist Wheel of Life
*Firmly held in a demonic grip, this Tibetan Wheel of Life is divided
into six sections, each representing a possible realm of rebirth.*

A Japanese Ghost
*Visitations from spiritual realms can arouse great terror. In this
Japanese woodblock, a ghost returns for vengance on his murderers.*

illusion of permanence. Buddhist gods, or *devas*, are also
held within *samsara*, the endless cycle of rebirth.

The Christian concept of heaven drawn largely from
descriptions in the New Testament Book of Revelation
combines the astrology and cosmology of ancient Greece
and Rome with Jewish images of the Lamb. It presents a
vision of God and Christ enthroned, surrounded by
saints, elders, angelic hosts and the multitude of the
redeemed. The heavenly realm offers believers a
prospect of eternal, immutable bliss, in contrast to the
finite, material realm of the Earth, which will be

destroyed in an eventual Apocalypse. Yet in Judaism the
relationship of the "World to Come" with the material
world is less clearly defined. The sacred Jewish writings
in the Talmud contain many references to the soul's
afterlife, and emphasize the importance of informed
preparation: "This world is like a vestibule before the
World to Come. Prepare yourself in the vestibule that
you may enter the hall." Yet whether the World to Come
is to be seen as a separate realm, or whether it describes
a resurrection of the dead in this world, depends upon
the individual believer's interpretation of the Talmud.

SPIRIT HELPERS

The idea of leaving our physical world for an uncharted spiritual realm arouses fear of the unknown in all of us. Even cultures that believe that the soul regularly visits other realms during its time on Earth regard these wanderings as dangerous, particularly for those without special knowledge or guidance from personal spirit helpers. The shamans of North America or Southeast Asia frequently undertake "soul flights" to the spirit world in search of healing wisdom or a lost soul. On such journeys, which transcend space, time and personal identity, the shaman depends upon spirit helpers to ensure his or her safety and success.

The Annunciation

In the New Testament, God usually chooses to communicate through his angels. In this 15th-century painting by Fra Angelico, the Virgin Mary is told by the angel Gabriel that she is pregnant with the Son of God.

The belief in a form of benevolent spirit, able to guide the soul in transit or to initiate the journey itself, is integral to shamanic practice. However, the notion occurs too in many other systems of belief. Angels (see page 122) assume the role of intermediaries between God and human beings in several religions, often appearing in dreams to sound warnings or give advice. The Hebrew Bible names only Gabriel and Michael, who respectively reveal the future and combat the forces of evil. In Christian tradition, the angelic hierarchy becomes more complex, and every individual is described as having his or her own protecting angel: "Take heed that ye despise not one of these little ones; for I say unto you, That in heaven their angels do always behold the face of my Father which is in heaven." The Koran describes several instances of the Prophet Muhammad's encounters with angels. In one of the most famous, Jibreel (Gabriel) brought the Prophet a supernatural creature called the Buraq, a winged mule with the face of a woman. Jibreel then accompanied Muhammad, mounted on the mule's back, on his miraculous night journey (*al-isra'*), in which they first flew from Mecca to Jerusalem, then ascended into the heavens. Here the Prophet was instructed by the Voice of God before returning to Earth.

The philosophers of ancient Greece also drew upon the concept of spirit helpers. Plato's *Symposium* describes them as envoys and interpreters, who not only carried prayers up to heaven, but also descended with commandments and

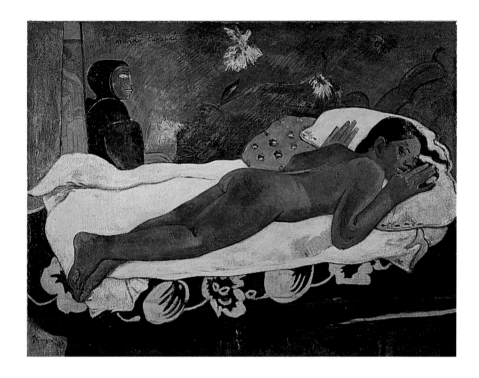

Manao Tupapau ("The Spirit of the Dead Keeps Watch")
Paul Gauguin's painting of 1892 portrays a beautiful Tahitian woman lying on her bed. She is watched over by an older woman in black, possibly representing her ancestor spirit.

responses from the gods. According to Plato, every human being possessed a spirit, or *daemon* – a fiery spark from the original world soul. The power to guide or instruct was invested within every *daemon*, but its advice could be heard only by those pure of spirit. Plato's conviction was echoed by the words of a Huichol shaman, Pedro de Haro, who said that to see spirits required only a pure soul.

Shamans may gather an astonishing variety of helper spirits during the early years of their long apprenticeship, and an intensely personal relationship often develops over time. Guardian spirits usually reflect the nature of the land: those of the Inuit peoples may be water creatures, such as seals or walruses, or even a polar bear whose body seems to be in flight as it glides through the water. The Plains Indians believed that shamanic spirit helpers took the forms of buffalos or eagles, endowing the shamans themselves with strength, vision and speed. Flight is associated with the release of the spirit from the limitations of matter, and many spirit helpers were said to travel on the wind. Shamans from the rainforest tribes often use plants with narcotic powers to achieve their visionary trances and transform themselves into a jaguar, fish or bird. For many of these *vegetalistas*, plants such as the hallucinogenic *ayahuasca* are thought to be spirit teachers. By ingesting the qualities of these spirits, the shaman also incorporates the plants' properties, and his or her own identity merges with that of the helper. Yet a degree of separation remains, and the spirits need to be respected if they are not to abandon the shaman or even become malign.

Griffins
A griffin is the mythological offspring of an eagle and a lion. It is said to guard the Tree of Life or the path to salvation.

STEALERS OF THE SOUL

Almost all spiritual traditions consider our souls to be essentially vulnerable. Without careful instruction and preparation, they may become lost on the voyage to the underworld, or afterlife; if found morally deficient, they may be devoured by monsters or subjected to endless torments. Demons, anxious to steal human souls for their own purposes, have appeared in all cultures, whether as pernicious external influences or more sophisticated manifestations of our unconscious minds. To Western eyes, some of the most terrifying demons have been those discovered in our own soul, or psyche, threatening madness or violence and destroying our true identities.

The human world is often perceived as "permeable", infused by malign, benevolent or amoral spirits from another realm. In the Shinto religion, the *kami* who govern almost all aspects of nature and human existence

St Zeno Exorcizing the Daughter of Emperor Gallienus
In this painting by Francesco de Stefano Pesellino, a Christian bishop is exorcizing a woman by commanding her evil spirit to abandon its possession in the name of Jesus.

include *oni*, or demons, who may cause many human problems. Some *oni* assume the form of animal spirits that are able to possess humans; if this occurs, the *oni* must be formally exorcized by a priest. However, *oni*, unlike demons of other faiths, are not regarded as totally evil: Shinto belief considers both "rough" and "gentle" qualities to be present in all phenomena, which may display either aspect according to circumstances.

The need to create and preserve spiritual boundaries in response to this perceived threat manifests itself in several cultures' rituals. Protected space, such as sacred sites of worship or the domestic sanctuaries of hearth and home, is defined by the uncontrollable forces outside it – the province of ghosts, demons and evil spirits seeking to capture living souls. Such creatures often represent the souls of human dead, unable to leave the physical world because of evil actions undertaken in life, or excessive attachment to a particular place. Sacred rituals attempt to contain or negate the influence of deceased souls. The Hindu period of *pitrpaksha*, for example, is a time for memorial rites (*shraddhas*) designed to pacify the souls of the deceased and honour ancestors, while the Shinto tradition venerates dead family members as *kami* and supplicates them with offerings of food. In Africa, the spirits of those who have died are known as the "living dead", and are regarded as still part of the family. When they are eventually forgotten, after several generations, the ancestors become unknown ghosts who if harnessed by sorcerers may cause harm to the living.

The soul is believed in several traditions to be particularly susceptible to evil influences in sleep, when it might wander from the body and be lost. Many cultures fear the *succubus*, a female spirit who is said to steal the

Lucifer

Lucifer is one of the many guises of Satan, the Judeo-Christian adversary of God. Once the greatest of God's angels, Lucifer started a rebellion and was thrown out of heaven. This painting by the Brazilian artist Alexandre Filho shows Lucifer, tied to a lizard, waiting outside a church. The surrounding apples may be a symbol of humankind's fall from grace.

Voodoo Charm

Voodoo, a religion widespread in Haiti, is a blend of Roman Catholicism and West African religion. Devotees believe that the world is populated by loa (spirits), who may favour, or harm, humans. Charms are carried by believers to ward off evil spirits and promote success.

semen of men as they sleep to procreate further demons. The terrifying, blood-sucking vampire, which appears throughout the world in widely diverse systems of belief, is often thought to strike at the defenceless soul of its victim under the cover of night.

Physical and mental illnesses have long been attributed to supernatural causes. Many beliefs possess rituals of exorcism designed to release the weakened soul from a malevolent power. Inexplicable diseases of the mind, such as epilepsy, were particularly feared, and associated with diabolic possession. The synoptic Gospels (those of Mark, Matthew and Luke) include instances of exorcism as part of Christ's wider healing ministry, and the formal rite is still included in Christian doctrine.

DREAMS AND VISIONS

The Visions of Ezra
Seven visions received by the Prophet Ezra from the archangel Uriel are related in the Apocrypha, an appendix to the Old Testament.

Since Sigmund Freud published *The Interpretation of Dreams* in 1899, the images that we experience while we are sleeping have been widely regarded in the West as subconscious references to our past. For thousands of years, however, dreams were believed by many cultures to be the most common vehicle for divine revelation.

Some societies believe that during sleep the soul enters a parallel world, which is as real and meaningful as our waking existence. In Malaysia, Senoi children are told that dream monsters have no power to hurt them unless they run away. They are taught to cultivate "dream friends", who help them conquer such adversaries. These friends might give the child a gift, such as a poem or song, to bring back into consciousness. When the child wakes, he or she is encouraged to recite it.

When dreams were frequently understood to have been sent by the gods, their interpretation was of great importance. The earliest records of dreams, incised on clay tablets and collected into interpretive dream books, were produced in Babylon and Assyria at the end of the 4th millennium BCE. The *Epic of Gilgamesh*, the legend of the tyrannical King of Uruk written in the Akkadian language during the 1st millennium BCE, is punctuated by dreams. Two of Gilgamesh's dreams presage the arrival of a man from the forest, who has been created by the gods to kill the king. When the man, called Enkidu, arrives, the two fight. Although Gilgamesh wins, he respects the strength and courage of his foe so much that the two subsequently become friends and together go on to accomplish great deeds.

In ancient Egypt, people seeking divine guidance would take herbal medicines before sleeping in the temple. On waking, their dreams would be interpreted by the priest. This practice of dream incubation was adopted by the Greeks, who built more than 300 shrines to serve as dream oracles. Because dreamers believed that they were visited by the gods, the sick frequently went to the shrines, hoping to be aided by Asklepios, the god of medicine. However, not everybody shared their confidence. Homer, in the *Iliad*, was the first to suggest that not all dreams were divinely inspired; he made a distinction between true dreams, which came through the "gates of horn", and dreams that cheat with empty promises, which came through the "gates of ivory".

Divine revelation by means of dreams and visions provides a common thread through many of the great religions. In the Hebrew Bible, dream sequences play a prominent part in the stories of Jacob and Joseph, which tell of the founding of the 12 tribes of Israel and their migration to Egypt. The Koran is believed by Muslims to be the literal word of God, transmitted to the Prophet Muhammad in a series of visions. The birth of Christ is heralded in a dream to his father Joseph. King Herod, the wise men and the shepherds also experience dreams and visions during the Nativity.

In the East, particularly in Buddhist and Hindu thought, sleep was seen as a type of consciousness similar to that experienced after death. It was said that in the dream state, an extremely fluid "mental body" existed which was not tied down to physical laws and could therefore encounter a wide variety of experiences.

States of consciousness after death were believed to be even more fluid. Teachers pointed out that if it was difficult to retain self-awareness and memory during sleep, then it would be even more difficult to maintain them after death. Dream yoga was therefore developed as a way of training the mind in preparation for death, and practitioners would try to maintain awareness through the various levels of sleep.

In the West, the role that dreams can play in providing access to our inner thoughts, needs and desires has been subject to much recent study. Carl Jung taught that, while dreaming, people may encounter ancient symbols that have remained active in the unconscious mind. Called the "archetypes", these symbols can be found in all the world's myths and religions.

Some psychologists believe that the depression and "loss of soul" which are so widespread in modern civilization are in fact the response of the mind to loss of contact with the religious in modern life. Dreamwork is a way of re-establishing that contact.

Vishnu Dreaming on Anata
In Hindu cosmology, the god Vishnu dreams on the back of the serpent Anata between the destruction of one world and the creation of the next. In this 17th-century painting, Vishnu is shown with his consort Lakshmi. The upper panel depicts (from the left) Vishnu riding on his celestial mount Garuda; Brahma; and Shiva.

COMMUNICATING WITH THE GODS

In many of today's native cultures, it is believed that the gods are active in reaching out to the human realm. They may show themselves in the power of elemental forces (such as thunder or wind), the movement of the heavens or the seasonal growth of crops; and their immanence gives inspiration and meaning to rituals of worship. The direct intervention of deities in human affairs informed several of the earliest religious traditions, from the Greek gods' participation in the Trojan wars to the divine status accorded to ancient Egyptian pharaohs. The manifestation of the divine in the human world has also entered into all the major monotheistic beliefs. Yahweh, the God of the Hebrew Bible, is described as revealing himself in the world through a series of miraculous actions, such as parting the Red Sea to allow the Israelites' passage, and inscribing the Ten Commandments on the tablets of stone given to Moses. In Hindu tradition the seventh and eighth avatars of Vishnu – Rama and Krishna – appeared on Earth to defeat evil and restore harmony; their victories are celebrated in the sacred texts of the *Ramayana* and *Mahabharata*. The possible number of Vishnu's incarnations is considered to be infinite, in contrast to the Christian perception of Jesus as the saviour whose single, momentous act of personal sacrifice redeemed all future believers.

Modern religions seek to communicate with their gods through prayer, petition and praise. The smoke of incense, for example, is thought by Daoists to transport prayers up to the gods. Other systems of belief rely upon the mediation of a spirit community – an African legend recounts how God became so irritated with the ceaseless demands of humankind that he withdrew into the

St Francis Receiving the Stigmata
Marks of the five wounds inflicted on Christ during the Crucifixion have appeared on the bodies of certain saints. In this fresco, painted by Giotto at the end of the 13th century, St Francis is shown at the moment of receiving the stigmata: rays of light stream from the wounds of Christ, piercing the saint's feet, hands and side.

celestial realms, leaving the spirits to deal with their requests. Shamanistic beliefs recognize spirit powers everywhere in their immediate environment: the Inuit sea spirit, known as Sedra or Nuliajak, governs the sea and sends out animals for hunting, while Sila the air spirit controls rain, wind and snow. The spirits are feared by the Inuit as the source of foul weather and misfortune in hunting. Attempts to placate them include ritual incantations and the wearing of masks and amulets. The Inuit also traditionally seek to ensure that the souls of hunted animals are returned to the spiritual realm by thrusting the inflated bladders of all the previous year's prey through holes in the ice. The souls may then re-emerge in the following year's quarry.

Buddhist Prayer Wheel

A prayer is written on a scroll and put inside the wheel. The prayer is made each time the wheel turns.

As well as propagating the rules for successful hunting, shamans cure disease, assisted by their spiritual helpers who communicate healing powers. Headdresses and masks play an important role in the process. Certain healing ceremonies among the Navaho peoples involve direct impersonation of the gods by masked performers. The masks, representing a group of gods called the *Yei*, are consecrated and "brought to life" through offerings of food and spirals of sacred smoke.

The imperial sacrifices to heaven conducted by Chinese emperors in the famous Temple of Heaven in Beijing sought to communicate directly with the spiritual realm. The emperor offered prayers for a successful harvest in his capacity of heaven's representative on Earth. They were uttered in the Qiniandian ("Hall of Prayer for a Good Harvest"), which reflects the geometric structure of the heavenly realm in a circular dome supported by brightly coloured beams. The temple's architecture served to reinforce the close relationship between heaven and Earth, and to strengthen the effect of the sacrifice.

Hinduism perceives the physical realm to be infused by a divine presence. Simple wayside shrines appear beneath trees, by rivers, in fields or even by street lamps in towns. Such shrines facilitate impulsive communication with the gods – offering a prayer or small gift – as well as longer worship. Integration of the sacred with everyday life is very important in Hindusim: cows, for example, may wander the street unharmed and revered, the symbol of the gods' benevolence. Divinity is manifested and worshipped in many natural forms, such as rocks, mountains, rivers, ford crossings or *tirthas* (see page 108), trees and plants. The ritual invocation of "Ram, Ram", a common greeting and early morning utterance among Hindus, acknowledges the role of the divine in the unfolding events of the day, and celebrates the miraculous gift of material existence.

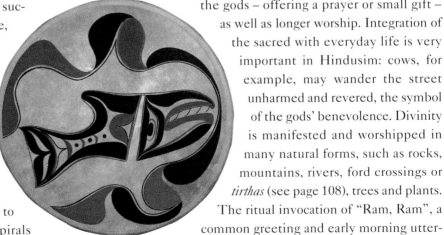

A Shamanic Drum

Drumming is frequently undertaken by shamans to summon the spirits.

TURNING-POINTS OF THE YEAR

In acknowledging the closeness of spiritual and material realms, we emphasize the importance and sacredness of the border regions between them. We may encounter these boundaries in many ways during our lives, perhaps through the confused perspective of a dream or the strange awareness of another presence when we appear to be alone. Many traditions have used certain moments of transition in the year as a focus for our relationship with other worlds. Dawn and twilight, the natural borders of day and night, have also long been recognized as ambivalent times when reality is blurred and sacred rituals acquire particularly intense spiritual power.

In Celtic belief, the boundaries between the seasons were periods of immense spiritual importance when divisions between the different realms became permeable. The great festivals of Beltane and Samhain were celebrated respectively in the spring and autumn, the seasons of the year held to be most auspicious for divine supplication. The night before Samhain, the Celtic New Year, is now known as Hallowe'en: poised between the old and new years, it is still viewed as an occasion when normal laws and demarcations are suspended. The doorways between the spirit world and the material world were thought to open, admitting both the souls of the ancestors and, potentially, evil spirits. Offerings were traditionally made to the visiting souls, and some Celtic countries retain the Hallowe'en custom of laying an extra place at the table for visitors from "the other side". Fires and lights in the home were traditionally extinguished at Samhain, briefly plunging the whole community into complete darkness. Sacred flames were taken from bonfires lit on mountain tops (see page 22) to rekindle hearth fires, restoring light and protection.

Hallowe'en

Jack-o'-lanterns are a relic of the bonfires that were once lit on the last day of the Celtic year.

The Hindu festival of Divali, which marks the New Year for many communities, is also closely associated with light. Oil lamps burn in homes throughout the night to invite Lakshmi, the goddess of wealth, into their midst and deflect the threats of darkness, misfortune and death. Restless spirits must be propitiated at Divali, and the god of death, Yama, pacified; cows, too, are honoured as symbols of fertility and prosperity, while firework displays celebrate the regenerative triumph of light over darkness.

New Year is recognized in many spiritual traditions as the time for sweeping away all the accumulation of evil from the old year. This process is celebrated in customs of ritual purification – extinguishing fires, fasting, and expelling demons or evil spirits. The concept of the scapegoat – an effigy who symbolically assumed the sins of an entire community, and who was then slaughtered or cast out into the wilderness – recurs in several New Year ceremonies. In the Balinese New Year, which falls in March, sculpted images from the temples are purified in the sea or in sacred springs. Animals are sacrificed, and ornate offerings placed to entice prowling spirits, which priests then exorcize with powerful mantras. The boisterous exorcism is often a communal affair, celebrating the natural resilience and regeneration of the human spirit.

Village Festival in Haiti

*The 20th-century artist Inatace Alphonse's painting of a street party in Haiti vibrantly portrays the
spring celebrations that still occur in agricultural communities.*

PERILOUS JOURNEYS

Voyages that involve great danger are a common theme throughout world religions and mythology. Many believe that such journeys are an allegory for the progress of the soul: that it is only through leaving behind all worldly possessions and attachments that we can learn our true worth, and that we must conquer our deepest fear – often death – if we are to achieve serenity.

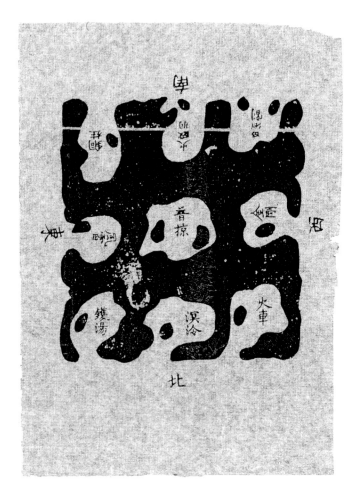

Heroes of epic voyages are often reluctant. On his way home from the Trojan War, Odysseus offended the god Poseidon and was cursed to wander the seas for ten years. The hero was not able to return to Ithaca until he had confronted the dark spirits of the underworld, who advised him on how to escape from his endless journeys.

Many cultures have tales of gods and mortals visiting the underworld to try to defeat death. The Greek myth of the musician Orpheus, who visited Hades to try to win back his wife Eurydice, is mirrored in the Shinto tale of Izanagi and his sister and wife, Izanami. These deities parented the Japanese archipelago and a series of gods and goddesses. When Izanami died giving birth to the God of Fire, her grief-stricken brother journeyed to the Land of the Dead to retrieve her. When he looked at his sister's decaying face, however, he fled in horror.

Perilous journeys rarely resolve themselves as the traveller wishes or expects. In the *Epic of Gilgamesh*, the Sumerian hero visits the underworld to learn the secret of eternal life. He succeeds, but the plant that offers everlasting youth is eaten by a serpent, and Gilgamesh returns to his kingdom accepting his mortality. In the Celtic *Voyage of Bran*, the hero and his 26 companions are lured to the underworld. After many adventures, they return to Ireland, but when the first man sets foot on land, he crumbles to dust. Bran learns from a stranger on the shore that 300 years have passed since they set sail.

A Daoist Map of the Underworld
Maps of the underworld could be studied during life, to aid the soul's journey. They could also offer warnings of the soul's possible destination after death. This Daoist map from 12th-century China shows the nine purgatorial chambers of the soul in the underworld.

Journey to the Underworld

*The Classical belief that the underworld was bounded by water is portrayed in this ancient
Greek fresco, which shows a newly released soul diving toward the realm of the dead.*

Journeys to the underworld are considered to be fraught with danger. Nevertheless, they are sometimes attempted by shamans or other spiritual leaders who wish to gain wisdom for their followers. At the heart of a shaman's initiation is an encounter with death in the form of ceremonial annihilation and rebirth. The ordeal often includes a ritual flaying by the spirits, who are said to remove the shaman's flesh from his bones and tear his eyes from their sockets. During the ordeal, the shaman receives his spiritual power from divine beings in human or animal form, to be used for the welfare of the tribe.

Many traditions state that the underworld borders our own world and can be entered through a cave-mouth, lake, volcanic crater or barrow mound. Others tell of a land located beneath the ocean or beyond the seas. The Chumash people in California believe that the Land of the Dead is separated from this world by a body of water: the soul must cross the bridge, avoiding water monsters on the way. Preparation for death while living – in the Chumash's case, by participating in hallucinogenic rituals – is believed to increase the soul's chances of making a successful transition to the underworld.

ANGELS

Deriving their name from the Greek *angelos*, meaning messenger, angels have traditionally assumed the role of intermediaries between spiritual and human realms. They feature in the Jewish, Christian, Islamic and Zoroastrian faiths, bringing divine revelations, as well as intervening in human affairs and acting as guardians.

The heavenly beings are divided into nine choirs, or hierarchical orders, ranging from seraphim, who are in direct communication with God, to angels, who are closest to humankind. Although each choir has a different form, all have wings. Angels may have evolved from the winged Greek goddess Nike, or Victory.

The Archangel Gabriel
Gabriel, whose name means "Strength of God", was an archangel, together with Ariel, Uriel and Michael. In Islamic belief Gabriel (Jibreel) heralded the revelation of the Koran to Muhammad.

Choirs of Angels
The celestial hierarchy or "choir" of angels has often been artistically interpreted in musical terms. Hans Memling's 15th-century painting Five Musical Angels *portrays the harmony of heaven.*

The Angel of the Apocalypse

One of the seraphim, the order of angels that guards the throne of God, the Angel of the Apocalypse has three pairs of wings: one to fly, one to cover its eyes from the glory of God and one to conceal its feet. In this

13th-century fresco from Anagni Cathedral in Italy, the fiery seraph is portrayed with stigmata – the wounds received by Christ on the cross – that take the form of all-seeing eyes.

Cherubs

Cherubim were the second order of angels, throne-bearers of God; "cherubs" such as the plumb little babies in Bouguereau's The First Kiss *(above) are more closely related to the Roman god of love, Cupid.*

HEAVEN

The belief that a just and devout life enables our soul to enter paradise after death is the promised reward of most Western religions. Heaven in the Bible or the Koran is usually portrayed as a beautiful garden filled with peace, beauty and love. However, each of us also carries a deeply personal concept of the afterlife, which may change during the course of our earthly lives. Some visualize a happy land filled with loved ones who have gone before; others believe that they will become part of a great cosmic energy. Many Eastern religions describe several heavens, which form temporary homes to the gods and deserving humans. However, such realms are still positioned within the endless cycle of rebirth, and so are considered inferior to nirvana.

Buddhist Heavens
Buddhists believe there are six heavens in the World of the Senses, the first sphere of existence, which also includes the human world. This mural depicts the Buddha preaching in the Tavatimsa Heaven.

The Peaceful Kingdom
Dora Holzhandler is one of many artists to portray (left) the vision of heaven described by the Prophet Isaiah in the Bible (Isaiah 11.6): "The wolf also shall dwell with the lamb, and the leopard shall lie down with the kid; and the calf and the young lion and the fatling together; and a little child shall lead them."

Stairway to Heaven

Many people who have undergone near-death experiences have described ascending a flight of stairs, similar to the vision of Jacob's Ladder in the Hebrew Bible, toward a bright light. Often a distant figure of a person or angel has been waiting to greet them.

Muhammad Ascending to Heaven

This illustration from a manuscript in Topkapi Palace in Istanbul depicts the Night Journey, one of the most important episodes in the Koran. It tells how Muhammad was woken by the Angel Jibreel and taken on a winged animal, "smaller than a mule but larger than an ass", first to the ruined Temple of Solomon in Jerusalem and then to heaven, where he received the commandments to pray from Allah.

HELL

In early cultures, hell was simply the abode of the souls of the dead. As such, it was neither a pleasant land, nor a place of punishment, but a shadowy, subterranean world, ruled by the dark lord of death. The ancient Greeks believed that the dead went to Hades, a vast cavern inside the Earth, where the dead heroes dwelt in the Elysian Fields, but the wicked were punished in the infernal regions of Tartaros or Erebos. The concept that hell was reserved for those who had led a sinful life was honed by later cultures, culminating in the Middle Ages with the Christian Church's graphic descriptions of the punishment meted out to sinners.

Christ's Descent into Hell
The ancient Near Eastern and Greek myths of deities and heroes visiting the underworld recur in the New Testament. This 17th-century Russian icon shows Christ, having died, descending into hell to deliver the righteous.

The Damned in Hell
The Christian view of hell, as captured in the late 15th century by the Master of the Palantes Altar, was a dark and foul-smelling prison, where sinners were tortured for all eternity.

Mictlantecuhtli
Aztecs believed that all souls, whether good or bad, had to pass through the dangerous underworld of the god Mictlantecuhtli.

Guan Gong Judging the Dead in Hell

In this Daoist illustration, the judge Guan Gong is presiding over a court in hell. Having examined the report on a person's life, he may reward them or, if they have sinned, punish them. In the foreground, various methods of torture by hell's demons are pictured, including flaying and dismembering.

An Ethiopian Image of Hell

Many cultures, especially those of hot, dry countries such as Ethiopia, imagine hell as a fiery realm where sinners are punished by burning. In Northern Europe, where extreme cold is dreaded, hell may take on a freezing aspect.

The relentless pressures of our modern lives are focused primarily upon material success. Spiritual beliefs offer us an alternative vision of existence, in which the limitations of such a perspective are transcended by the potential of the soul. Faiths possess many different aspects: some may celebrate the sacredness of the natural environment, while others seek to renounce the illusion, or *maya*, of the physical world. Many systems of belief seek to draw us into a more profound understanding of ourselves and our place in the universe. The disciplines of meditation, prayer, retreat and vision quests demand perseverance and dedication from the student, and a teacher's wisdom and

SOUL AND TRANSCENDENCE

experience are often essential in guiding us toward our spiritual goal. In attempting to reach an inexpressible absolute, whether it is called paradise, or nirvana, or a name more personal to ourselves, we pay tribute to the highest aspiration of the human spirit.

FAITH

Developing and preserving a spiritual faith may not be a comfortable path. In acknowledging our belief, we are often called upon to relinquish material success and rational, scientific beliefs to focus instead upon a deeper, more abstract reality. The philosopher Kierkegaard described the immeasurable "leap of faith" made by those of us who embark upon such journeys – the conviction that is strong enough to enable us to "remain out upon the deep, over seventy fathoms of water, still preserving the faith". Even fundamentalist beliefs, which appear to offer rigid certainties, still require the individual to question his or her worthiness for salvation in the eyes of God.

Faith is particularly important in the major monotheistic religions of Judaism, Islam and Christianity, with their emphasis upon God's eventual, irrevocable judgment of each human soul. Even within a single religion, faith is not a fixed concept, but may change in emphasis over time; in Judaism, for example, the Torah interprets faith to mean an immense *trust* in God, rather than – as now – a belief

Handprints of Satis
The above handprints were made by Hindu widows who immolated themselves on their husbands' funeral pyres as an act of faith.

Jonah and the Whale
In the Bible, Jonah is swallowed by a whale (right) when his faith fails and he tries to escape from carrying out God's commands.

in his very existence. All three religions believe that the divine presence is manifested through sacred scriptures, which record the history and nature of God's covenant with his chosen people. Such texts, conveying the Word of God and describing encounters with him, are integral to the rituals and tradition that inspire personal belief. This individual spiritual faith is more than an intellectual conviction; it is a passionate, emotional commitment that may often be counterpointed by agonizing doubt.

The power of faith is indisputable: individuals throughout history have been prepared to sacrifice their most valued possessions, including their lives, as a result of their trust in God. The Islamic obligation of *jihad*, literally translated as "striving" in the service of Allah, requires physical defence of the faith if necessary, without regard for personal safety. Many spiritual traditions celebrate those who confronted the challenges of their beliefs: Abraham's faith in divine will, for example, led him to countenance the otherwise intolerable action of sacrificing his own son (see page 62). The heart of Christian belief lies in the death and miraculous resurrection of Jesus, through which his followers may hope to be redeemed if their trust and repentance are sincere. Christian martyrs who have died for their faith are often venerated as the recipients of divine strength and power.

Communion Chalice
Transubstantiation, in which Communion wine is transformed into the Blood of Christ, is essential to Catholic faith.

In contrast to the monotheistic religions, the faith of many Eastern beliefs is less focused on divine textual authority. Even the most holy writings of Buddhism, for example, are considered "mere pointing at the Moon" – indications of a truth that can only come from personal experience. In Hinduism, the spiritual goal of *moksha*, or liberation from the cycle of rebirth, may be pursued through the paths of knowledge, action or devotion. The third of these, *bhakti-marga*, involves a complete surrender of the ego to the mystical experience of divine grace and power. Knowledge of the deity thus emerges *through* faith rather than itself inspiring spiritual conviction.

Faith and doubt are inextricably linked in spiritual experience. In his teachings the Buddha acknowledged the limitations of blind faith, requiring that his students should always test his words. The Zen Buddhist tradition believes that three elements are needed to make spiritual progress: great faith, great doubt and great perseverance. Faith is required to discover and trust the inherent truth of Buddhist teaching; doubt to challenge and overcome superficial understanding; and perseverance to continue despite distracting hopes and fears. In recognizing the complexities and hardships of a spiritual path, our religions and beliefs also celebrate the enduring human determination to overcome them.

THE DEFEAT OF SUFFERING

We all encounter periods of misery that defy us to discover a deeper meaning or purpose in our lives. Yet most spiritual beliefs, far from avoiding one of faith's most difficult tests, do offer both explanations and solutions for our distress. Some religions may regard suffering as an intensely personal experience that we may paradoxically use to strengthen our faith. Other traditions consider it a symptom of an all-embracing and illusory human condition that our souls may overcome by recognizing ultimate truth. Reconciling a universal order with the apparently arbitrary distribution of grief in the world is a challenge, yet we all know people who are able to accept suffering as a feature of existence and who accommodate it within a broader spiritual perspective.

In Hindu belief the individual soul, or *atman*, is linked to the ultimate reality of *brahman*, the vital essence of the cosmos. Full recognition of this correspondence is equated with the supreme Hindu goal of *moksha*, a spiritual liberation from the endless cycle of rebirth that characterizes human existence. Suffering arises from an inability to recognize the reality of *brahman*, together with an excessive attachment to worldly wealth, pleasure and emotions. Such egotism, founded upon illusion, ignores the responsibility that everyone bears for maintaining cosmic order, or *dharma*, on which Hinduism's ethical base is constructed. According to the law of karma (see page 28), behaviour in one life will continue to have repercussions in future reincarnations. Through virtuous conduct and the defeat of egotism, the soul may advance through a series of lives toward spiritual perfection. If it cannot shake off material attachments, however, or continues to commit evil actions, it will remain permanently trapped in a spiral of suffering characterized by unhappiness and greed.

The teachings of the Buddha emphasize our need to confront the reality of *duhkha*, meaning transience, mutability and decay, that essentially defines human existence. In recognizing suffering as an inescapable facet of our lives, Buddhists seek to transcend the craving for illusory pleasures and security that paradoxially anchors people more firmly in the miseries of the world. True defeat of suffering in Buddhist eyes demands acceptance

The Scourging of Christ
This painting by Giotto depicts Christ being scourged, or whipped, before his crucifixion. Christians believe that Christ had to suffer and die on the Cross to redeem the sins of humankind.

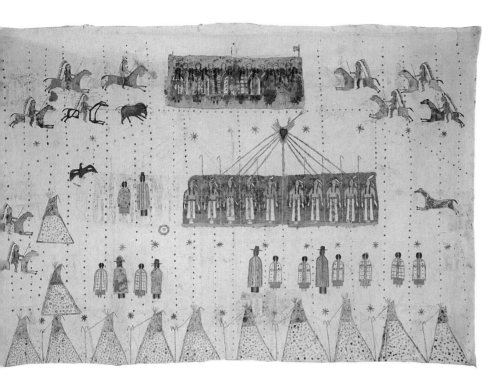

The Sun Dance
In this Plains Indian painting of a Sun Dance (left), the dancers are pictured hanging from thongs fixed to their chests. They believed that their suffering would ensure that the world would be renewed and that a plentiful supply of buffalo would be guaranteed for the coming year.

The Buddha at the Moment of his Enlightenment
Images of the Buddha, such as this huge statue in Burma (Myanmar, below), remind his followers that they can only escape suffering by attaining nirvana.

of its inevitability through meditation techniques that still the spinning mind. In the Mahayana tradition of Buddhism, the highest spiritual achievement is to become a *bodhisattva* (see page 149) – one who continues to participate in the world's sorrows in order to bring others to enlightenment.

The monotheistic religions of Judaism, Islam and Christianity all acknowledge the existence of earthly suffering within the dominion of a just and all-powerful God. This paradox is partly explained by the concept of the divine retribution or reward that will be meted out to the individual in a life after death; the Jewish Talmud, for example, contains many references to such redress. However, Judaism ultimately recognizes suffering to be rooted in divine mystery, and thus beyond the scope of human rationalization: "It is not in our power to explain either the wellbeing of the wicked or the sufferings of the righteous," observes the Ethics of the Fathers.

Christianity perceives Christ's suffering on the Cross and subsequent eternal resurrection to be the divine response to human misery. By sharing in the feelings of anguish endured by Christ in his Passion, a believer may be brought closer to the Godhead. Transient suffering on Earth is set against the hope of an enduring redemption.

PENITENCE

As well as adhering to the law of the state, each of us follows a personal code of behaviour and sometimes also a set of religious rules. If we break any of these rules, we may be haunted by guilt and shame. Many find that by feeling remorse for our past sins or mistakes, we allow the healing power of penitence and atonement to enter our hearts and purify our spirits.

The importance of recognizing and confessing one's sins, and of being forgiven, has long been acknowledged in the Judeo-Christian tradition. The Jewish calendar

Imayat Khan Dying
This 17th-century painting shows an emaciated man dying from opium abuse. Islam teaches that Allah forgives those who truly repent of their sins.

features an annual season of penitence, marked by important festivals at the beginning and end. Rosh Ha-Shanah is the Jewish New Year and is heralded in the synagogue by the high plaintive sound of the ram's horn calling people to prayer. The liturgy of Rosh Ha-Shanah puts human life in the context of a greater reality by focusing on the kingship of God and asking him to reign in and over each and every Jew. The festival is the first of ten days of penitence, during which time true repentance is said to be especially acceptable to God. The tenth day is Yom Kippur, the Day of Atonement. Atonement derives from "at-one-ment", and signifies that through true repentance of the heart, men and women can recover their original union with the sacred.

Yom Kippur celebrates the day that Moses came down from Mount Sinai with the second tablets of stone, on which God had commanded him to recarve the Ten Commandments. Moses brought with him the good news that God had pardoned his people for worshipping the golden calf, a false idol. Since then, Yom Kippur has been a day of fasting and self-denial, but it is also a joyful occasion because it reaffirms God's covenant with his chosen people.

In the Roman Catholic Church, penance is one of seven sacraments and deals with the forgiveness of sin after baptism. Early forms of penance

Mary Magdalene
Mary Magdalene has traditionally been portrayed by the Church as an errant sinner whose soul was saved by Christ.

involved sinners making a public confession and incurring severe penalties. Because penance was allowed only once in a lifetime, those guilty of serious sins would often put it off until their death was near. In the light of this, in 1215 the system of confessing to a priest at least once a year was introduced. The priest would give absolution to the sinner and order him or her to carry out "penances". At first these punishments could be very harsh; later they were commuted to simple prayers or even donations.

Abuses of the confessional were instrumental in causing the Reformation, and today most Protestants make a standard congregational confession at morning or evening prayer. The Anglican version reads: "We have left undone those things which we ought to have done; and we have done those things we ought not to have done; and there is no health [holiness] in us."

Showing remorse for our misdeeds is an important stage along our spiritual path. By truly recognizing our improper actions and vowing never to repeat them, we put them behind us, and move on with new lightness of heart and spirit.

The Jewish Shofar
The shofar, *a ram's horn, is sounded on Rosh Ha-Shanah, marking the start of the Jewish New Year and heralding the ten days of penitence and the Day of Atonement.*

VISION QUESTS

The Holy Grail
This illustration from a Flemish illuminated manuscript of the mid-14th century depicts Josephe, the son of Joseph of Arimathea, conducting mass for the first knights departing on the Holy Grail quest. Christ is portrayed within the Grail itself, with blood pouring from his wounds into the cup.

Most of us at some point feel that our lives lack purpose, but few of us seek, or desire, to be given a task by the divine. However, there are some – shamans, mystics and great teachers – who have crossed the threshold between the physical and the spiritual worlds, seeking salvation for themselves and others. The search for spiritual knowledge or revelation is known as a vision quest and may involve life-endangering practices such as fasting, drug-taking, self-mutilation and blood-letting. Those on a quest might learn a song with special meaning, see a vision of the future of the tribe, or find inspiration to lead others on their spiritual journey.

One of the most famous Western vision quests is the legendary search for the Holy Grail. Believed to be the chalice used by Jesus at the Last Supper, in which Joseph of Arimathea later collected the blood of Christ, the Grail first appeared in medieval French stories associating it with King Arthur's court. In later tales, the knights of the Round Table pledged to search for the Grail and then embarked upon a series of trials and initiations, from which many did not return. The trials, set by mysterious figures along the way, sought to test the worthiness of each knight's soul, and to expose the conflict between worldly attachments and a true love of God. Only four knights – Lancelot, Perceval, Bors and Galahad – succeeded in seeing the Grail and only one, Galahad, participated in its mysteries. The Grail quest still exerts a powerful fascination as a resonant symbol of the soul's search for spiritual wholeness and salvation.

Many of the world's major religions owe part of their central message to the vision quests of their founders. After his baptism, Christ may have undergone the initiation rites required by the Nazarene and Essene religious communities. The New Testament relates how he wandered alone in the desert, fasting for 40 days and 40 nights. Having refused to be tempted by the devil, Christ returned with a new vision for humanity.

Muhammad too went alone into the hills, where he encountered the archangel Jibreel (Gabriel), who pronounced that he, Muhammad, was to be Allah's messenger. The Prophet then spoke what Muslims believe to be the actual words of Allah, as recorded in the Koran.

A Shamanic Vision Quest
This "yarn painting", fashioned from dyed wool, was produced by the Huichol people of western Mexico. It depicts the spiritual journey of an antlered shaman.

Jaguar
Amazonian shamans closely identify themselves with the jaguar. They may assume the animal's form on a vision quest.

Vision quests are an important feature of Native American culture. Shamans communicate with the spirits after fasting and bathing in a sweat lodge. Returning from their interior journey, they bring back counsel and healing for the tribe. Black Elk, a Sioux Indian who died in 1950, had a great vision when he was nine years old, in which he was shown the incredible beauty of the world and entrusted with the sacred task of keeping alive the spirit of the Earth. In his old age, frail and blind, on the summit of Harney Peak, he admitted that he had not been able to keep to his promise and that the sacred tree, whose spirit he had been entrusted to keep, had never bloomed and was now withered. He offered prayers to the Great Spirit, asking that if even a small root lived, it should be nourished so that it could bloom and birds again sing on its branches. Black Elk believed his vision quest had borne no fruit. Yet, years after his death, stories about his vision are widely known and the message that was revealed to him by the Great Spirit, about the preciousness of Mother Earth, is still alive and inspiring a new generation of people. His vision quest has become active in the modern world.

TOWARD NON-ATTACHMENT

Eastern spiritual traditions emphasize the solitary path of the wandering ascetic or *sannyasin*, a person who has retired from society and devoted himself or herself to spiritual realization through meditation and surrender. The search for the *atman*, or soul, begins by withdrawing into the "cave of the heart". *Sannyasins* abandon all attachments, such as family ties, power, money, ambition and even existing religious duties. Hindus encourage and support these wandering holy men and women, as they believe that the mystic is to the community what the soul is to the body, giving it life and inspiration.

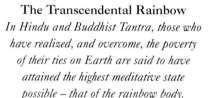

The Transcendental Rainbow
In Hindu and Buddhist Tantra, those who have realized, and overcome, the poverty of their ties on Earth are said to have attained the highest meditative state possible – that of the rainbow body.

Both the Buddha and Mahavira, the respective founders of Buddhism and Jainism, were renowned ascetics. While the Buddha taught the Middle Way between materialism and renunciation, Mahavira believed that release from the endless cycle of rebirth required complete abandonment of the material world. From the moment of his renunciation he went naked and showed no interest in food, water or sleep.

Merely letting go of physical attachments does not mean that the internal psychological dependence ceases. A Zen story tells how two novices were walking beside a stream when they met a beautiful girl, unable to cross because of her delicate robes. One of the monks carried her across, but was admonished by his companion who pointed out that monks were not supposed to go near women, especially beautiful ones. The reply from the first monk was: "What is the matter with you? I left the girl on the bank, but you are still carrying her."

The great monastic houses of Christian Europe imposed strict vows of poverty, chastity and obedience on those who took holy orders. For some this was a life of torment, while for others it offered a gateway to total freedom of the spirit: confronted with the absolute love of God, all worldly concerns slipped away. St John of the Cross urged contemplatives to seek to enter into Christ's being in complete nakedness, emptiness and poverty. Summing up the way in which to imitate Christ, St John declared: "To reach satisfaction in all, desire its possession in nothing. To come to the knowledge of all, desire the knowledge of nothing. To come to possess all, desire the possession of nothing. To arrive at being all, desire to be nothing."

This fundamental renunciation of the spirit would have been understood by the ancient Daoist sages of China. They believed that to act in accord with the *Dao* (the Way), people needed to discover stillness of heart, to overcome ceaseless desire and ambition, and to live in harmony with nature. Loss, decay and death were considered no less essential than gain, growth and life. The Daoists sought not to influence these cycles of change, but to swim along with the currents of life, like a fish in water. Their philosophy was to avoid any action that required calculated, ambitious strategy. Many sages renounced all wealth and ambition to live in the mountains among the clouds and pine trees. Here they cultivated supreme non-attachment, their mirror-like minds reflecting a parade of phenomena, but retaining nothing.

A Jain Diagram of the Universe

*In the Jain universe, the World Axis (Mount Meru) is surrounded by seven oceans, seven continents and
the heavens. Jains cultivate a profound aesthetic of non-attachment in their search for spiritual truth.*

MEDITATION

The Sufis – Islamic mystics – say that knowledge without spiritual practice is like a tree that does not bear fruit. The discipline of meditation allows the practitioner to live more fully in the present moment with awareness and peace. Religious traditions teach many different forms of meditation, giving ordinary people the opportunity to attain genuine spiritual experience. However, recalling the mind from its habitual chaotic turmoil to quietness and solitude – "the still point of the turning world" – is central to all.

Meditation, or *dhyana*, is the penultimate limb of Raja Yoga, one of the most famous Hindu philosophical traditions. It was first written down in Patanjali's *Yoga Sutra*. The essence of Hindu meditation is illustrated in the following stanza from this classic handbook: "Yoga consists in the intentional stopping of the spontaneous activity of the mind stuff." The mind is likened to the surface of a lake ruffled by the wind. The purpose of yoga is to cause the wind to subside and allow the waters to return to stillness. When the wind blows, the waves break and distort the reflections so that they can be seen only as a broken image. When the water is calm, the whole reflection of the sky and clouds appears distinctly and the depths of the water are translucent and clear. This serene image is likened to the self realized through yoga. Using meditation, we are able to settle down the

Kali Yantra

The Hindu goddess Kali – the female embodiment of eternal time, who both gives and destroys life – is the focus of this yantra. *Practitioners meditating on this aspect of the goddess are reminded that all worldly attachments and ambitions are ultimately futile.*

myriad thoughts that splinter our concentration, and so are left with a clear picture of our true self and our place in the world.

In Christian mysticism there is a tradition of formless meditation – the aim of which, according to St Francis, is to achieve "a loving, simple and permanent attentiveness of the mind to divine things". Mystics of this tradition aspired to be in the presence of God, rather than becoming one with God. St John of the Cross said that the soul should be allowed to remain in rest and quietude, in which, through patience and perseverance, without any conscious activity, the presence of God would be found. In order to attain freedom of the soul, it was necessary for the mystics to "liberate themselves from the impediment and fatigue of ideas and thoughts".

Internal thoughts and emotions block direct intuitive experience. This blockage maintains the illusion of self, preventing connection with the divine. Meditation provides a space in which attention is brought back again and again to the simple yet profound reality of being. Rather than promoting an unhealthy introspection, it may, if properly executed, release energy that has been locked in shackles of anxiety. Meditation can bring relief from the continuous whirlpool of our thoughts, offering the soul an ability to live fully in the present moment, and to discover a deep delight in the everyday world.

Hatha Yoga

Whereas practitioners of Raja Yoga reject the body as a useless tool of illusion, Hatha yogis see the body as an instrument of release. This illustration from an 18th-century yogic textbook (left) depicts a Hindu ascetic performing one of the asanas, *or postures, recommended for meditation.*

Shri Yantra

The archetypal yantra *is the Shri Yantra (above). Its pattern evokes the sacred union of Shri, a manifestation of the Goddess Shakti, with her male aspect, Shiva. The* yantra *is composed of nine superimposed triangles: the ones pointing upward are symbols of the male god Shiva, while the downward ones represent the female energy of the goddess. At the* yantra's *centre the dot, or* bindu, *symbolizes the Absolute.*

PRAYER

When we pray, we are petitioning, or communing with, the divine, perhaps in search of inspiration, guidance or comfort. Prayers may also be said in response to fear: when placed in extreme danger many who consider themselves atheists find themselves praying.

The simplest prayers are those that ask for assistance during important episodes in our lives such as childbirth, coming of age, marriage, war and death. In many cultures – for example, in ancient Greece – there were a great number of deities to whom one could pray, each of whom had an area of responsibility. Nike would be invoked for victory in war, Poseidon when crossing the sea, Hera for easy childbirth, and Demeter for an abundant harvest.

Some Christian prayers were adapted from more ancient petitions to pagan gods or, in the case of the type of Irish prayer known as the "Ionica" or "breastplate", elemental forces. One of the most famous, St Patrick's Breastplate, opens: "I arise today, Through the strength of heaven: Light of Sun, Radiance of Moon, Splendour of fire, Speed of lightning, Swiftness of wind, Depth of sea, Stability of earth, Firmness of rock."

In Eastern religions, such as Hinduism and Jainism, *mantras* are used in prayer. The *mantra* is a short word or syllable (such as "*Om*") that encapsulates a form of cosmic power and so is considered sacred. The word *mantra* has the Sanskrit verb *man* (to think) as its root, and as an instrument of thought it is used to protect the mind from wandering into its usual discursive channels.

Christ as the Saviour
Although the Christian Church forbids idol-worship, icons – such as this 13th-century painting from Mount Athos – are a focus of prayer and meditation for Orthodox Christians.

The Eastern Orthodox Church places a strong emphasis on meditative prayer. One of the most familiar supplications, the Jesus Prayer, is used in a way similar to a *mantra*. The words are simple: "Lord Jesus Christ, Son of God, have mercy on me, a sinner." Apparently an ordinary form of petitionary prayer, this formula was in fact used to effect changes in the consciousness. The prayer was said aloud for a specific number of times, then repeated silently at intervals during the day and night. Finally, the chant was taken down from the "head" centre of consciousness to the "heart" centre where it was thought to live with every heartbeat. In monasteries, monks would repeat the prayer while counting knots on a cord.

Rosaries are used as an aid to prayer in many of the world's religions. Sikhs repeat the divine name, *nam*, while counting the beads on a *simarani* (rosary); Muslims say one of the 99 names of Allah that appear in the Koran while turning their prayer beads; members of the Pure Land sect of Chinese Buddhists use a rosary when reciting the name of a deified Buddha such as Amitabha; and Christians, particularly Roman Catholics, say prayers while counting the beads of their rosary, normally 50 in total, divided into groups of ten.

It has often been said that a holy fool is closer to God than a learned scholar and that it is purity of intention that makes prayer effective. A story from Tibet illustrates that notion. One day two erudite monks were looking down from their monastery on an old man making the circuit of the sacred places, followed by a beautiful woman whom they recognized as Tara, the deity of compassion. The monks asked for the man to be brought to them and questioned him. The man amused them by his apparent stupidity: he knew nothing about Tara's following him, but was just reciting the prayers as he had learned them. When he repeated the prayers to the monks, they ridiculed his mistakes and taught him their correct methods. The next day, looking out of the window, they saw the old man, this time alone. Once more the monks summoned him and, with humility, told him to return to his old ways, for his simple devotion obviously had the blessing of Tara. Soon afterwards, the old man was seen whispering his imperfect prayers, followed once more by the radiant figure of the goddess.

Islamic Prayer Beads
One of Allah's 99 names should be recited on each of the 33 beads in this string, as the chaplet is turned three times.

A Male Ascetic
This mid-17th-century Rajasthani painting (right) depicts an ascetic at prayer.

RETREAT

A Map of Mount Athos
When the threat of oppression lifted, many early Christians entered monasteries, such as the Orthodox communities on the Mount Athos peninsula in Greece. The island's first community was established around 961. By the 14th century there were some 40 monasteries, 20 of which are still in use.

As the stresses and distractions of modern life increase, many of us find that we lack the necessary space and calm for spiritual growth. By making regular visits to monasteries, ashrams or other places of religious retreat, we are responding to an inner call for solitude to restore the balance between the sacred and secular in our lives.

The first Christian hermits retreated to the Egyptian desert during the 4th century CE, fleeing persecution. There they lived simple lives of prayer and meditation in loosely organized communities. Many of the monks fasted, and some attempted more rigorous feats of endurance – such as standing for hours in the desert sun, living at the top of columns or walling themselves up in caves – to try to detach themselves from the physical

world. St Isaac of Syria explained their motives when he said: "A man who wishes to become excellent in God has first to wean himself from the world, as a child is weaned from his mother's breasts."

Following in the footsteps of Muhammad, who spent long periods meditating alone in the desert, many Sufis – members of a sect of Islamic mystics – considered retreat to be the most important of all spiritual disciplines. Early Sufis believed that every person had a human and a divine soul, which competed for nourishment. It was only by denying the human soul, through renunciation of the pleasures of life, that the divine soul could flourish. A Sufi would often stay in his cell for several weeks, repeating the divine name, Allah, continuously or "until he had no breath left". It is said that some Sufis obtained sudden illumination almost immediately, others after some weeks, but the retreat was judged to be successful only if the vision remained undiminished after the Sufi had re-entered everyday life.

Many Tibetan monasteries are perched precariously on cliff edges, but devotees on a retreat often seek even more desolate places, in the mountains. One of the most celebrated Tibetan Buddhist saints was Milarepa, who renounced his early life as a practitioner of black magic to live in the caves of the Himalayas. At first he was given supplies of food and clothing, but as these dwindled he realized that he could live without them. Using yogic techniques to keep warm and relying on nettles for nourishment, he was content with his life of meditation. On hearing that he was near to starvation, his sister came to visit him and was horrified by his appearance. By his own account, Milarepa's eyes had sunk in their sockets, his flesh was green from his diet of nettles and his coarse grey hair streamed from his head in a flood. The food that his sister provided allowed him to go further with his meditation, and he achieved total enlightenment. A song that he sang listed everything that he had abandoned in his mountain cave – including endless dialectics, illusions of ignorance, hope and fear, the need to please relatives and friends, doctrinal politics, conceptual forms of meditation, hypocrisy and his own fear of death.

Milarepa
This 17th-century Tibetan statue depicts the hermit yogi Milarepa (1040–1123). He started his career as a magician and became a great Buddhist lama *(teacher).*

Milarepa never became a monk, but many who did also carried out extreme forms of retreat. A Buddhist monk could be walled up in a small cell for years, cultivating his inner vision so that at death, when the mind and body separated, he would not be in a state of bewilderment, and so could be sure of a favourable rebirth.

Many people, finding the distractions of normal life constricting, have gone on retreat only to be terrified by the silence and desolation. Romantic visions of the joy of living a simple and harmonious life amid the beauties of nature have often been destroyed by the shock of being alone or the pain of being unmasked. Such discoveries may be spiritually useful, as they encourage those on retreat to appreciate that not everyone can seek enlightenment through this particular path. Great saints such as Milarepa overcame the human need for society; wedded to isolation, they found that solitude gave them the psychological space in which to further their spiritual development.

Christian Troglodytes
Early Christian monks hollowed out churches, chapels and small cells in the volcanic rocks of the remote Anatolian region of Cappadocia.

ECSTASY AND TRANSFORMATION

One of the most famous fables collected by the ancient Greek author Aesop is that of the tortoise and the hare. The moral of the story is that the slow but steady student is more likely to win the day than the more gifted but undisciplined pupil. Life, however, teaches us that many advances are inspirational, rather than natural progressions in a line of thought. Although most religious traditions emphasize the importance of a gradual spiritual development through prayer or meditation, they recognize that ecstatic or visionary states can lead to sudden leaps in faith or understanding. Such states can be self-induced, by taking hallucinogenic drugs or listening to mesmerizing sounds, or may also occur spontaneously.

St Teresa of Avila was renowned for her ecstatic visions: she said that she was visited by a beautiful angel, whose face seemed to be aflame. In his hands was a golden dart, the tip of which was on fire. The angel plunged the arrow into her heart, causing a pain so great and so sweet that it made her moan, and left her aflame with the great love of God. The physical power of St Teresa's raptures could raise her whole body from the ground.

The Church explained her experiences by saying that ecstasy was not a special gift but a consequence arising from the weakness of the human frame, which could not bear the force of divine action. St Teresa herself believed that raptures and visions were merely side effects and that it was unhealthy to become attached to them. She and her pupil St John of the Cross taught that the mark of spiritual understanding was not the degree of bliss that a person experienced or how much he or she loved God, but how much he or she was able to love other people.

While St Teresa's rapture was unusually strong, many Christians have experienced speaking in tongues, a form of ecstatic speech. The first report of this phenomenon in the New Testament tells how, after the ascension of Christ, his followers were visited by the Holy Spirit and began speaking in other languages.

Many religious traditions have produced maps of the spiritual path and show altered states of consciousness as stages on the journey. The value of transcendent states is that they provide a powerful vision of reality beyond day-to-day consciousness. Buddhist teachers recognize the different levels of rapture that can occur, but argue that they are not necessarily signs of spiritual progress. The rapture starts as small, pleasurable vibrations within the body, and becomes increasingly intense as it resonates outward. It is often accompanied by a spontaneous release of physical tension that gives rise to involuntary movements. Those who enter a transcendent state may experience a change in their sensory perceptions. The Buddha reminded students

St Teresa's Visions
In Christian symbolism, fire is a manifestation of the Holy Spirit. When describing her ecstatic visions, St Teresa of Avila recounted that an angel pierced her heart with the flaming arrow of divine love, causing her to swoon.

Dionysus

This mosaic of c.180 CE is from the House of Masks on Delos. It shows Dionysus, the Greek god of wine and altered states, riding on the back of his sacred animal, the leopard, whose skin was believed to have magical properties.

that the purpose of his teaching was not to attain such blissful states but to unlock the warmth and profound compassion of the heart. However, Maharishi Mahesh Yogi, the founder of the Transcendental Meditation (TM) movement, taught that this energy, if properly channelled, could liberate human consciousness.

In shamanic societies, trances or ecstatic states are entered in order to seek help and advice for the tribe from the spirit world. The shaman journeys on a magical flight, which may have been attained by spiritual means alone, or may have been induced by drumming, dancing or taking hallucinogens such as hashish, mescaline or fly agaric. On the journey, the shaman has a transformed vision of reality; if successful, he or she may gain knowledge of the life-force that pervades the universe and gives coherence and energy to all things.

The distrust felt in many modern societies toward altered states of consciousness also existed in ancient Greece. There, when people were drunk, acting or in a state of religious ecstasy, they were believed to be in the realm of Dionysus, whose rites were associated with excess and madness. His most famous followers were the bacchantes, a band of frenzied women who were said to tear apart animals and humans during their orgiastic revels. Today, most of the religious traditions that include a form of ecstatic practice remain outside the mainstream, and the value that can be gained by entering a transcendent state is often questioned in the light of the dangers that can be involved.

TEACHERS OF FAITH

Most of the world's religious traditions require us to develop great spiritual knowledge and understanding to overcome obstacles on the path. Although certain outstanding people may be able to undertake such a journey alone, most of us need a skilful teacher to direct, stimulate and encourage our awakening. Living spiritual traditions seek to transmit knowledge to the students without losing the inspiration and impact of immediate experience. Under the guidance of an experienced teacher, we begin to see beyond the realm of everyday concerns to a world of vast and profound wisdom.

Spiritual development in the major monotheistic religions – Judaism, Islam and Christianity – is linked to knowledge of sacred, divinely inspired scriptures that establish the tenets of the faith. All believers are encouraged to read and reflect upon these texts, but each religion also regards teaching as an essential function of its spiritual leaders. Modern rabbis, for example, combine the roles of preacher, pastor and counsellor with their scholarly study of the Torah – the sacred teach-

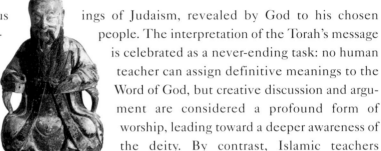

Lao Zi
This 16th-century Chinese carving depicts Lao Zi, who is credited with founding Daoism.

ings of Judaism, revealed by God to his chosen people. The interpretation of the Torah's message is celebrated as a never-ending task: no human teacher can assign definitive meanings to the Word of God, but creative discussion and argument are considered a profound form of worship, leading toward a deeper awareness of the deity. By contrast, Islamic teachers demand a rigid adherence to the Koran, which they believe contains the literal words of Allah. In Muslim eyes the Koran provides the authoritative, final statement of Allah's unchanging purpose, following the earlier scriptural revelations of the Torah and the Gospels. Religious devotion thus places great emphasis upon learning the Koran by heart, a process forming the basis of Islamic instruction.

Christians regard Jesus as the supreme teacher, the inspiration for all preachers of the faith, and the Gospels as the vehicle through which his doctrines are expressed – often in the vivid parables and aphorisms that characterize Jewish teaching. Jesus's first students were his disciples who, according to the synoptic Gospels, eventually came to understand, teach and seek to enact the doctrine that was taught and practised by Christ.

Spiritual teachers are viewed as extremely important in Hinduism, which offers various paths of worship toward its ultimate goal of *moksha* (see page 132). The devotee is offered choices between the three paths of knowledge, devotion and action, depending on his or her occupation, personality and particular stage of life that he has reached – student, householder, hermit or ascetic.

Christ and his Apostles
Christ's first 12 disciples were chosen to spread his message. Judas, who betrayed Christ, does not appear in this 13th-century image.

Buddhist Arhats
In the Theravada school of Buddhism, arhats *are enlightened beings who have cut the ties of* samsara *(the endless cycle of rebirth) and will never be born again. The* arhats *pictured in this Tibetan image are Ajita and Pindola Bharadvaja.*

Both the path of knowledge (*jnana-marga*) and that of devotion (*bhakti-marga)* are usually undertaken with the guidance of a *guru* – a personal spiritual guide, considered in certain Hindu schools of belief to be a god, who assists the student throughout his or her journey. Some devotional, or *bhakti,* traditions, in which the ego is surrendered to discover the deity through the senses and emotions, perceive reverence for the teacher's wisdom as integral to a student's spiritual fulfilment. Indian philosophers and holy men are also venerated as teachers through the inspiration of righteousness and humility that they offer to the world.

Buddhist teaching is structured upon the formulation of the Four Noble Truths, or *aryasatya*, recognized by the Buddha on his enlightenment. The Truths explain the pervasiveness of *duhkha* (meaning transience, impermanence and universal decay) in all human life. They propose the Eightfold Path – a combination of ethical behaviour, meditation and skilful action – as a guide to transcending *duhkha*.

As the Buddhist tradition developed, the role of the teacher changed. The first *arhats* or "worthy ones" – the spiritual ideal of the Theravada school – emerged from among the Buddha's original followers after his death. In the later schools of Mahayana Buddhism, strong emphasis is placed upon compassion, with the teacher taking a very personal involvement in the life of the student. By contrast, in the Vajrayana and Zen schools compassion took on a fierce quality, using methods of unconventional and seemingly harsh treatment to force the student into experiencing reality directly. Many celebrated Mahayana and Vajrayana teachers are viewed as the incarnations of great *bodhisattvas* (see page 156).

THE PATH OF RITUAL

Rituals, both sacred and secular, pervade every aspect of our lives, easing us through unfamiliar or difficult situations, and giving structure to our positive experiences of faith. A ritual's origins are often lost to us, with the result that many habitual actions – such as shaking hands when we first meet somebody – may seem senseless if examined. However, many rituals are re-enactments of a society's sacred myths, and so may contain symbolic forms or archetypes that communicate directly with our psyche or soul.

The Chinese philosopher Confucius believed that his country was in a state of moral decline owing to a general lack of ritual at all levels of society. Although no book of rites exists from Confucius's time, guidance is provided on ancestor worship, mourning rules and sacrificial ceremonies in the later *Li Ji*. Ritual was believed to preserve harmony between heaven and Earth, and the emperor was invested with the unique responsibility for ensuring the success of the empire by making sacrifices in the Temple of Heaven in Beijing (see page 37). Confucius believed that aspects of ritual could be applied to everyday situations to strengthen individuals and their families.

Guru Nanak, the founder of Sikhism, placed less emphasis on ritual than most other spiritual traditions, believing it could impede communication with God. Sikhs do, however, recognize and celebrate five rites of passage: the birth of a child, the bestowing of a child's name, the coming of age, marriage and death.

As well as the ritual observances of prayer, fasting, alms-giving and pilgrimage, Islam recognizes two "official" Holy Days. 'Id al-Fitr, the Feast of the Breaking of the Fast, ends Ramadan. The most important day in the calendar, however, is 'Id al-Adha, the Great Feast, which celebrates Ibrahim's willingness to sacrifice his son Ishmael. On this day, every Muslim should ritually sacrifice a *halal* (lawful) animal such as a sheep, goat, cow or camel.

Many Jewish rituals originated with the 613 precepts of the Torah. Each of these divine commandments is known as a *mitzvah*. The obligation to keep the precepts begins when a boy reaches the age of 13 and a girl the age of 12, hence the terms Bar Mitzvah and Bat Mitzvah for the Jewish coming-of-age ceremonies. The Sabbath and the Passover, two of the most important Jewish rituals, are acts of thanksgiving. Each week, the Sabbath essentially celebrates the creation of the Earth and remembers that God is present in everything. During the annual spring festival of the Passover, Jews give thanks for their safe delivery from Egypt. A ritual meal and service are held in the home on the first night of the Passover. Known as the Seder, it uses symbolic foods to remind Jews of their ancestors' ordeal, including unleavened bread, eaten by the Israelites on their journey; bitter herbs as a remembrance of slavery; a bowl of salt water standing for the tears of the oppressed; and a roasted bone symbolizing the sacrificial lamb.

The Great Mosque at Samarra
The dynamic spiral minaret of the 9th-century mosque at Samarra in Iraq reflects the desire of the soul to ascend to the heavens.

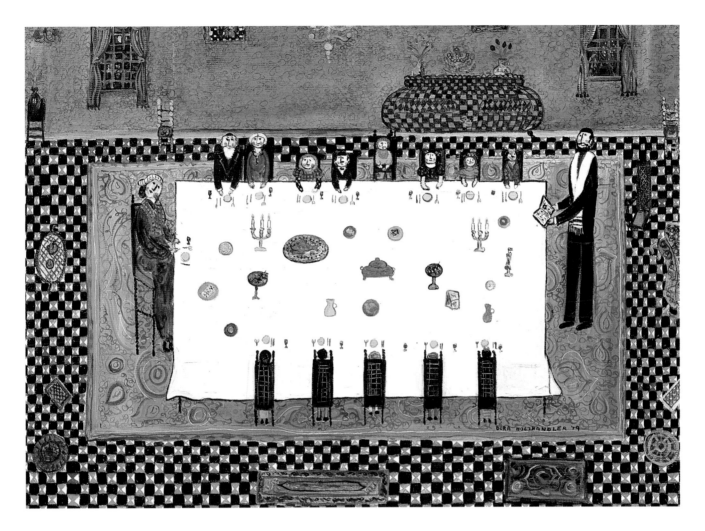

The Seder

The Passover Meal, by Dora Holzhandler, depicts the Seder, a meal and service held in the home on the first night of the Passover.

The Christian Gospels all suggest that the Jewish Passover was associated in some way with the first Lord's Supper, when Christ directed his followers to commemorate him by eating bread and drinking wine. Since then, Christians have ritually consumed these ancient symbols of body and spirit in the Communion.

Ritual answers a deep-seated human need and provides an opportunity to express the many complex longings and emotions that are part of the psyche. Ritual can ultimately convey devotion to the gods or gratitude for the pleasures of life; it may serve to acknowledge transgression or to articulate an overwhelming pain. Most importantly, it provides an awareness within us that our lives are part of a wider, more profound covenant: ritual is truly an occasion when the human and divine realms are perceived to meet.

THE EXCEPTIONAL LIFE

At some point in our lives, most of us will have contact with individuals whose spiritual knowledge and authority are greater than our own. Such figures, sometimes encountered within a religious context, sometimes met by chance in another walk of life, inspire respect and veneration in many cultural traditions. Their power may be manifested in diverse forms, including healing, skills of divination or a profound spiritual knowledge. However, the really exceptional lives belong to those who found lasting systems of belief, based upon the personal quests they have undertaken – often involving physical suffering – to discover true spiritual values.

The Buddha, born in Nepal in the 6th century BCE, was such a person. Renouncing his worldly role, he devoted much of his life to seeking an explanation of human suffering and finally achieved enlightenment beneath the Bodhi Tree at Bodh Gaya (see page 28). His subsequent teachings of *dharma*, or truth, offered to rich and poor alike, established an enduring legacy. The Buddha founded a community of monks, the *Sangha*, whose lives of meditation and material simplicity are devoted to maintaining the *dharma*. He continued to teach until his death, known to believers as *parinirvana*.

His near-contemporary Confucius established a spiritual philosophy in China that informed the country's beliefs for more than 2,000 years. Confucius emphasized that learning and moral development were both a personal responsiblity and an ethical gesture of reverence to heaven – the veneration of which he considered more important than the prevailing fascination with divination, spirits and ghosts. Confucianism set the spiritual focus firmly upon the individual, in a society that traditionally placed greater emphasis on communal life and maintaining the sacred harmony of heaven and Earth.

Islam's founder, the Prophet Muhammad, was born in Mecca in 570 CE. During a period of solitary meditation in a cave on a mountain near Mecca, Muhammad is believed by Muslims to have been visited by the archangel Gabriel, or Jibreel, who commanded him to

Death of the Buddha

This scene from a 17th-century Japanese handscroll (left) shows the parinirvana *(final extinction) of the Buddha. All those who remain within the cycle of rebirth – gods and demons, men and women, birds and animals – watch the event with humility.*

Muhammad Surrounded by his Disciples

Muslims believe that Muhammad was only a man, but that he lived a perfect life. Traditionally, the prophet's face is veiled as a mark of respect, as in this illustration from a 16th-century manuscript, the Fine Flower of Histories *(below).*

"recite in the name of your Lord". The Prophet began to utter the sacred words of Allah himself, which, together with those of his subsequent revelations, were written down as the Koran. The chief message of the Koran is the absolute supremacy of God; Muhammad is honoured in Islam as Allah's human prophet, the vehicle of the divine word and proclaimer of the true faith.

Jesus, by contrast, is considered by most Christians to be both God and man. He offered radical teachings on achieving salvation through God's forgiveness, as well as preaching the need for compassion and love on Earth. In a climate of messianic fervour, Jesus's charismatic ministry and concern for the poor were viewed as dangerous by the authorities, leading to his crucifixion.

PARADISE

Most of us believe that, in the present age, paradise cannot be attained while we are alive – although some say that it can be glimpsed. Many cultures agree, however, that humankind once dwelt in a luxurious paradise, close to the divine, and that our souls yearn to return there.

Paradise is usually described as a garden or park, often with a central tree or copse, a mountain at the garden's heart and rivers flowing outward in the four cardinal directions. Existence there was devoid of all earthly ills and was invested with total harmony and peace, as well as with a glorious awareness of the sustaining divine presence. Descriptions of paradise served as an example of how life could be lived and also as a promise of the soul's reward for a virtuous life.

Frequently the voyage to paradise involved crossing water, the symbol of spiritual regeneration. The Celtic paradise of Tir nan Og, the "Land of Youth", was the Promised Land of the West, set within the ocean, and the Russian paradise, Belovody, translates as "Land of White Waters".

In the Koran, it is written that the Gardens of Paradise are divided into four sections – those of the Soul, the Heart, the Spirit and the Essence – and that each is watered by crystal streams; golden pavilions line the shady banks; and the faithful recline at ease, drinking wine and embracing celestial *houris* (nymphs). The only word spoken there is *salaam* ("peace").

Ali Husein and Hasan in Paradise
The two grandsons of the Prophet Muhammad are depicted in paradise in this 17th-century Islamic miniature.

In Hindu and Buddhist systems of belief, paradise is seen not as an ultimate goal, but as a temporary state, subject to the universal conditions of change and decay. The great Hindu gods Brahma, Vishnu and Shiva are not considered to be immortal but are thought to enter the Wheel of Time at the end of each *yuga* (see page 21). Mahayana Buddhism teaches that "Buddha fields" may be created through the vast spiritual power of a Buddha or an advanced *bodhisattva*. Buddhist devotees may be favourably reborn into these gardens of spiritual bliss, where *dharma* may be practised and progress made toward full enlightenment. Sukjavati, the home of the Buddha Amitabha and the most famous of these fields, is pictured as a jewel-encrusted realm, with lotus flowers, the symbols of spiritual perfection and transcendence, rising in many colours from the clear mountain lake. Each blossom supports a Buddha, rapt in contemplation, while surrounding gods and goddesses play delicate musical instruments, accompanied by the sounds of rustling jewel trees.

The Garden of Eden is associated with paradise in the Judeo-Christian tradition: Jewish prayers for the dead contain an entreaty that the deceased's soul should

Garden of Paradise
*This 16th-century German perception of paradise shows the Queen of Heaven – the Virgin Mary – seated
in the Garden of Eden, the infant Jesus playing at her feet.*

rest there in a state of immortal bliss. This closeness to God, lost since the Fall from Eden after Adam and Eve ate the fruit of the Tree of Knowledge, is viewed as the soul's reward after a lifetime's striving for perfection.

Many of the world's great mystical traditions understand that the search for paradise is in fact an inner journey, which is fed by the desire to transcend the suffering and limitations of existence on Earth.

More than an actual location, however beautiful, the concept of paradise is a powerful symbol of peace within the human heart itself.

ENLIGHTENMENT

From our childhood, when the dark seems to be full of unknown terrors, we continue to acknowledge the power of light to conquer forces of darkness and evil. Many religions consider the ritual lighting of candles to symbolize spiritual transformation, from the darkness of ignorance and doubt to the revelation of living faith. In the Hebrew Bible, the Psalms often associate light with the soul's progress toward salvation – "thy word is a lamp unto my feet and a light unto my path". The command to kindle the flames of the Menorah (see page 96) has long been interpreted as an instruction to illuminate daily life with the sacred wisdom of the Torah. Enlightenment, literally meaning "being brought into the light", is the spiritual goal of many systems of belief – a deep clarity of perception in which truth can be comprehended through a conviction of both mind and heart.

The 18th–19th-century English poet William Blake wrote of the huge gulf between the actual and potential vision of humankind: "If the doors of perception were cleansed everything would appear to man as it is, infinite. For man has closed himself up, till he sees all things through narrow chinks in his cavern." Such a journey, from the relentless, claustrophobic prison of illusion to the liberation of unobstructed wisdom, is described in the Buddha's quest for enlightenment. In seeking a solution for the overwhelming presence of *duhkha* (roughly translated as impermanence and suffering, in all their diverse forms) in human life, the Buddha-to-be moved beyond the extremes of asceticism to belief in a middle way. He finally achieved enlightenment beneath the Bodhi Tree at Bodh Gaya in a single night, after defeating the weapons and temptations of the demon Mara. Challenged by Mara as to his right to occupy the seat beneath the Tree of Enlightenment, the Buddha-to-be gestured downward, requesting the Earth itself to bear witness to his worthiness. It responded with a tremendous earthquake, confirming the future Buddha's victory and enabling him to progress through the night to the final sequence of revelations.

In recognizing the cycle of *samsara*, which chains humans to rebirth, the Buddha-to-be also saw that as an individual's actions and their consequences were linked (the law of karma), spiritually correct action over several lives was the key to achieving release from this cycle. This understanding brought him to the perfection of becoming a Buddha ("One who is Awake"), whereupon he was able to transmute the three poisons of passion, aggression and greed. As the Buddha achieved nirvana (literally meaning "blown out", a state of being likened to the extinction of a candle), his accumulated wisdom composed itself into the Four Noble Truths and infinite compassion at the core of Buddhist teachings ever since.

Final comprehension of the Four Noble Truths is accessible only to a Buddha, and equates with the attainment of enlightenment and nirvana. However, the Buddha taught that anyone might embark upon the spiritual quest, and his early followers believed in four stages of enlightenment, ranging from an initial rejection of egotism and illusion to the ultimate realization of nirvana as an *arhat*, or "worthy one". Later traditions of Buddhism, such as the Mahayana and Zen, believed that the highest enlightenment lay in becoming a *bodhisattva* – "One whose Essence is Enlightenment" (see page 149). The *bodhisattva* ideal, that of world saviour, vowed never to seek nirvana until even the grass and the dust had achieved buddhahood.

The Journey to the Centre

*In many cultures, the maze is symbolic of the inner journey toward enlightenment. The path
is less likely to be lost if it is lit by the candle of knowledge.*

SACRED FIGURES

Every world religion reveres those of its members who have shown great spiritual strength and dedication during their lives. The actions of such men and women have often been used as examples of what it is possible, as a human, to achieve. Sometimes, the historical facts of a sacred figure's life have been elaborated and enriched with myth to produce a tale redolent with symbolism. Stories of the Christian saints, the holy ascetics of Hinduism, the ten gurus honoured by Sikhs, the Daoist immortals, Islam's mystical Sufis and the generous *bodhisattvas* of Buddhism serve as inspirational models for others on the spiritual path. Although sacred figures are rarely worshipped, their relics (bodies or possessions) are often thought to be imbued with holiness. Some are thought to have left traces on the landscape; thus, sacred footprints, places where monsters were slain and wells blessed by the saints all became magnets for pilgrims seeking a connection to the wisdom of the past.

Ma Gu
This Chinese painting on silk by Hsiang Kun shows the Daoist immortal Ma Gu. According to legend, Ma Gu was a beautiful sorceress who lived in the 2nd century CE. She used her magic to reclaim land from the sea, which she then planted with mulberry trees. Images of Ma Gu are given to couples on their silver and golden wedding anniversaries.

Guru Nanak
The founder of Sikhism, Guru Nanak (1469–1539) was born a Hindu in an area ruled by Muslims. He taught that meditation on the divine name could lead to escape from rebirth.

St Catherine of Alexandria
In legend, St Catherine is said to have lived during the 4th-century rule of Roman emperor Maxentius. She was tortured on a spiked wheel and beheaded for opposing the persecution of Christians.

Avalokiteshvara
One of the most popular Mahayana bodhisattvas, *Avalokiteshvara is revered as the embodiment of compassion. He is usually depicted with multiple arms, all of which he uses to dispense aid. The Dalai Lamas are sometimes said to be successive reincarnations of this* bodhisattva.

The Christian Evangelists
The four saints who wrote the gospels of the New Testament (Matthew, Mark, Luke and John) are depicted in the 8th-century Book of Kells *as winged beasts. In Revelation (4.7) they are described circling the throne of God: "And the first beast [Mark] was like a lion, and the second beast [Luke] like a calf, and the third beast [Matthew] had a face as a man, and the fourth beast [John] was like a flying eagle."*

MIRACLES

Myths and legends describe events that do not fit into the scientific, rational view of the world. Some stories are clearly allegories of the soul's journey, but others describe historical events by which the established laws of nature were said to have been overturned. Visitors to India and the Himalayan kingdoms have often returned with strange tales of supernatural powers: holy men who could walk on fire or water, levitate, change their shape and size or become invisible. For generations, incidences of prophecy, clairvoyance, telepathy and out-of-the-body experiences have been reported around the globe. The thirst for marvels remains strong today, and stories of

The Ascension of Muhammad
The Islamic miracle of the Night Journey tells how angels escorted Muhammad into the heavens and the presence of the Lord.

The Birth of the Buddha
The future Buddha is said to have emerged from the side of his mother, Queen Maya, shown in this 19th-century Tibetan bronze.

weeping statues, miraculous cures and heavenly visions are still a regular occurrence. Because they make people reassess their fundamental beliefs and encourage faith in a power that is greater than humanity, miracles have often been performed by spiritual leaders to assert their divinity or to reinforce the truth of their message.

Feeding the Five Thousand
Once, when preaching to 5,000 people, Jesus is said to have fed the crowd on two fish and five loaves of bread (right).

The Raising of Lazarus
The Gospel of St John tells how Christ proved his power over death by returning Lazarus to life. This painting by Giotto (left) shows Lazarus, wrapped in his grave clothes, emerging from his tomb four days after he had died.

The Buddha Walking on Water
In this panel from the east gate of the stupa at Sanchi (left), the Buddha is seen walking on water. He is said to have performed this miracle to convince Kashyapa of the truth of his message. He succeeded and Kashyapa became one of his leading disciples.

SACRED TEXTS

Although a few cultures still pass down their rituals and beliefs by word of mouth, most have a central text or texts that cover their history, law and spiritual convictions. In the case of the Hindu body of sacred writings, these can span hundreds of years, from the *Rigveda*, dating from *c.*1,200 BCE, to the *Mahabharata*, which was not completed until the 4th century CE. To avoid misinterpretation, there are authorized versions of sacred texts such as the Christian Bible, the Jewish Torah and the Sikh Guru Granth Sahib. Muslims believe the authority of the Koran to be absolute, as it gives the actual words of God. All sacred texts, however, are written in a highly symbolic form and have layers of meaning that are open to interpretation. They embody the sacred values of a culture and record the ancestry of the people and their precious relationship to the gods.

The Christian Bible
The Christian Bible comprises the texts of the Old and the New Testaments. Before the advent of printing, manuscripts were copied out by skilled monks and were often highly illustrated, or illuminated. This example shows the flight into Egypt of Mary and Joseph with the infant Jesus.

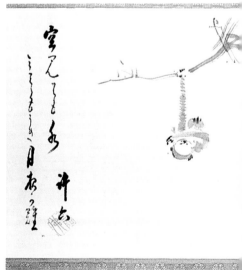

The Koran
The Koran is often embellished with ornate calligraphy (left); depictions of Allah are forbidden.

Zen Art
In Zen Buddhism, calligraphy and painting may be expressions of the sacred. The script (right) is by the 17th-century poet Matsuo Basho, the painting by a pupil.

The Dao
This Chinese character for the Dao, *which translates as the "Way" or "Path", refers to the undefinable principle that is responsible for creation out of nothing.*

The Hebrew Bible
Jews revere the name of God, and although it may be written down, as in this page from the Hebrew Bible (above), it is not usually read aloud.

The Torah
The Jewish law, or Torah, is written on scrolls, which are kept inside the Ark in the synagogue. A crown (right) is placed over each end of the scrolls to symbolize the sovereignty of the Torah over Jews.

BELIEF SYSTEMS OF THE WORLD

African (native) religions

Those religions in Africa that were not introduced by Islamic or Christian missionaries are generally animist: that is, they perceive spirit beings (including tribal ancestors) in local landmarks and other natural features, although some tribes also acknowledge deities of a higher order. Most rely on the mediation of a shaman or holy person who is able to travel into the spirit world in a trance to seek out the solutions to current problems or disorders. Many tribes have their own creation myth, often featuring a vast, primal serpent.

Alchemy

Alchemy, which originated in ancient Egypt and ancient Greece, allies chemistry and astrology to seek not merely the marvellous physical medium ("the philosopher's stone") that will turn base metals into gold, but also its metaphysical equivalent, believed to unlock the secrets of the universe – even of life and death.

Ancient Egyptian religion

The history of ancient Egypt spans more than two millennia (c.3000–300 BCE). A number of elements remained constant in Egyptian religion during all this time, although often given different names at different times: a creation story, involving the sky, the Earth, and the air between; the Sun god; the dualistic struggle between the good god Horus and the bad (but sometimes not too bad) god Seth; the mother goddess; and the afterlife. Deities often personified animals and their perceived characteristics; many were specific to a region or city. From early on, the pharaoh was also accorded divine status. Egyptian religion was in the hands of a powerful and wealthy priesthood, headed by the pharaoh himself.

Ancient Greek religion

Observance of ritual was the main function of Greek religion, even more than reverence for the many gods and goddesses of the pantheon, whose behaviour and intervention in human affairs were motivated by emotions such as jealousy, vengeance and lust. Well-established by c.570 BCE, the Greek pantheon included gods from many sources: major deities such as Apollo, the god of healing and music, and Artemis, the chaste goddess of the Moon and the hunt, were of non-Greek origin. Rituals overseen by priests and priestesses, including dramatic performances at religious festivals, brought the community common, unifying purpose, especially in hard times. The vast body of mythology included, in addition, folk heroes left over from pre-Hellenic times, such as Herakles (Hercules).

Ancient Roman religion

Religion in ancient Rome was compartmentalized: each deity was responsible for an aspect of daily life and was accorded prayer and supplication according to status and necessity. Worship might take place in the home, at a local shrine or sacred place, in a temple or, on feast-days, in a national stadium with the emperor or other dignitary presiding. The gods were thus "occupational", which made it easy to incorporate many foreign deities into the pantheon – either because they had an identifiably similar "occupation" or because the occupation was one for which the Romans had no current deity.

Australian Aboriginal beliefs

Fundamental to the beliefs of all Aboriginal peoples is the concept of the Dreaming, or Dreamtime – the time when the Sky Heroes or ancestor spirits formed the world and everything in it, from mountains and rivers to the organization of human society. Where those spirits left their mark, in unusual features of the local terrain, are the Dreaming tracks or "songlines". It is at the site of these songlines, or through spiritual connection with them, that present-day Aborigines can ritually participate in the Dreamtime, especially in relation to the spirit or animal that is their own tribal totem. Great reverence is paid to such sacred areas, of which the best known in the West is probably Uluru (Ayers Rock). Religious symbolism includes complex artwork and body-painting.

Aztec religion

The Aztecs combined as a people from several Central American tribes, all of whom seem to have had a history of being overtaken by severe natural disasters. The result was a strong religious belief that human sacrifice was the only way to avert such disasters in the future. Many of the large number of Aztec deities thus demanded human sacrifice on a regular basis and on an enormous scale, increased after episodes of warfare at which the Aztecs were so proficient. The priests wielded considerable power and possessed an extraordinarily precise calendar which was itself imbued with religious meaning.

Babylonian religion

Babylon was a city-state subject to domination over many centuries by a number of different peoples (including the Sumerians, Assyrians and Persians) who imported their own religious ideas and systems – all of which were duly incorporated in an extraordinarily diverse pantheon and scheme of ritual observance. The main consistent religious sentiment, however, was of reverence for agricultural deities, in particular Tammuz.

The great ziggurat, or step pyramid, at Babylon (model for the Tower of Babel and possibly Jacob's ladder – the Jews were exiled to Babylon) was part of a religious complex dedicated to the chief deity Marduk, god of the spring Sun.

Buddhism

The goal of Buddhism is enlightenment – release from the worldly physical and mental attachments of the body, and from the cycle of reincarnation by which one soul is reborn in a succession of different bodies, in order finally to merge with the infinite entity that is the Supreme Self. First to attain such enlightenment was Siddhartha Gautama, known as the Buddha, in India about 2,500 years ago, and it was he who set out the means by which enlightenment is achievable: the Four Noble Truths and the Eightfold Path. The original form of the religion is known as Theravada; the more evolved and liberal form is called Mahayana, which includes the notion that a *bodhisattva* may delay reaching the final stage of enlightenment in order to inspire others. Other forms of Buddhism are current in Tibet and Japan. Buddhism requires considerable self-discipline and asceticism, and to some extent is as much a philosophy or way of life as a religion.

Celtic beliefs

There was never a single Celtic religion: Celtic groups (from *c.*3000 BCE onward) revered their various deities on a strictly local and ancestral basis, and with appropriate rites. However, there were certain constant elements. For example, all Celts believed in an afterlife; many of the Celtic gods and goddesses were somehow triple or triune in nature; and there was an unusually high proportion of female deities. Many of the deities were intimately linked with the powers of nature – particularly with specific trees (notably the oak), with fire, with thunder and lightning, and with horses – or with the fearsome violence of warfare. Another element was a fascination with the idea of magic, especially in association with legendary locations.

Christianity

Christians believe that spiritual salvation is possible for all humans who sincerely believe that Jesus Christ ("Anointed") underwent formal execution by crucifixion on their behalf, to redeem their sins; that he physically rose from the dead two days later; and that he was the Son of God. Whether he was in addition also therefore the Messiah foretold by the prophets of Judaism remains shrouded in mystery, following the formal acceptance by Christian authorities four centuries later of the doctrine propagated by Jesus's major follower Paul. Rather than emphasizing the Judaic messianic tradition, Paul's doctrine developed the mystical concept of the Trinity: the belief that one God exists in three "Persons", of whom Jesus is one and the Holy Spirit another. Jesus's teachings were inspirational in both spiritual and social terms, but the plethora of differing interpretations over the centuries has led to a considerable diversity of Christian Churches and denominations. Many of these observe different forms of ritual, even in the most significant rite of Communion which commemorates Jesus's "Last Supper" before his crucifixion.

Confucianism

In Western eyes, Confucianism is not so much a religion as a philosophy of altruism by which people with authority, great or small, are required to strive for the happiness and wellbeing of those for whom they are responsible, the overall result to be as near as possible to "heavenly" perfection. Confucianism has thus contributed markedly to the social and political order of China for thousands of years after its institution by Confucius (Kong Fu Zi) in the late 6th century BCE.

Daoism

The major tenet of Daoism (or Taoism) is that there is a unity behind the multiplicity visible in the world, a connection between human affairs and the events of nature, and an overall balance and harmony in the cycles of life. The central beliefs of Daoism are expressed in the *Dao De Jing*, a book thought to have been written by Lao Zi in the 5th or 6th century BCE. By following the *Dao*, or Way, the devotee can seek spiritual contentment through experiencing oneness with the natural world. The Daoist ideal is *wu wei*, or non-action, a state of contemplation that is not intent upon any result.

Gnosticism

This esoteric, mystical form of philosophical faith developed in the Greco-Roman world in the 2nd century CE. It had the greatest influence on the young religion of Christianity, and stressed the redemptive power of esoteric knowledge achieved through divine revelation. The material world, into which humans had tragically fallen, was perceived as essentially evil and corrupt. Revelation of human origin, essence and destiny might be achieved only by intuiting the mystery of the self, rather than through intellectual study or scriptural reference.

Hinduism

Intertwined with the history and caste-categorized society of India over millennia, Hinduism propounds that the goal of spirituality is the final merging, after many successive human incarnations, of the individual soul with Ultimate Reality. Such a release (*moksha*) from the cycle of rebirth is attainable primarily through righteous conduct (*dharma*) and by the renunciation of worldly attachments. The Hindu pantheon contains a veritable host of deities, to any of which a person or a family may choose particular allegiance, although most Hindus worship one of three: Vishnu, the creator and protector of humankind; Shiva, the destroyer, cosmic dancer and symbol of male energy; or Shakti, the great goddess and female counterpart of Shiva. Rituals and practices vary greatly. Pilgrimage is common, and there are many regional and national festivals.

Islam

Muslims believe that the words of their holy book, the Koran, are the words of Allah (God the Almighty, the All-Merciful) himself, as revealed to the Prophet Muhammad – the latest and greatest of the holy prophets, of which Abraham and Jesus were earlier exemplars – during the 7th century CE. As the unchangeable words of God, they have to be learned and studied in their original Arabic, and obeyed with submission (one meaning of *islam* is "submission") and precise attention to ritual and ritual purity (including prayer five times a day facing Mecca). A righteous life, or a martyr's death, leads to paradise, often envisioned as a garden.

Jainism

Jainism originated in India in the 6th century BCE, around the same time as Buddhism. To Jains, every living being (humans, animals, insects, plants, even microscopic organisms) has a spirit or soul, and may over time, through successive incarnations, progress to and past the human stage, and eventually (by ridding itself of residual impurities such as worldly attachments) release itself from the cycle of rebirth and reach nirvana. Such potentiality means that all life must be regarded as sacrosanct and all forms of violence shunned. Some Jain ascetics and monks accordingly go naked apart from nose-masks (to avoid breathing in dust-mites), sweeping with a light broom the ground at their feet.

Judaism

An ancient religion, dating originally from the 2nd millennium BCE, Judaism was unusual for its time in being strictly monotheistic. From early on its adherents, known as Hebrews or Israelites, regarded themselves as the Chosen People of a single God who, by direct contact and through patriarchs and prophets, revealed laws of conduct (notably the Ten Commandments) by which all humankind might in due course – depending on God's judgment on the Last Day – find spiritual salvation. The Hebrew Bible contributed greatly to the traditions of Christianity, and to a lesser extent those of Islam; later writings and commentaries have since amounted to a significant body of religious teaching. Orthodox Jews follow an annual schedule of feasts and fasts; rituals are performed both in the home and at the synagogue. There is emphasis on ritual purity both in interpersonal relations and in diet.

Manichaeism

Mani, the founder of Manichaeism (*c.*240 CE), posited that the world, originally good, had become invaded by the evil principle. Within an esoteric framework of mythology – including elements of Gnostic Christianity – he declared that the release of goodness into the world would effect not only the original state of separation between good and evil but salvation for all in the resultant kingdom of Light. Adherents were required to conform to a highly ascetic regime of self-discipline.

Mayan religion

The Maya (*c.*300–900 CE) were an agricultural civilization in Central America to whom corn (maize) was by far the most significant crop. The religion thus focused partly on the corn god and other deities responsible for good harvests, and partly on gods inimical to humans and their wellbeing, such as those believed to bring floods and eclipses. Rituals (including sacrifices) in relation to both benevolent and malign deities were complex. The priests, who were accorded great power, were highly-skilled astronomers, who made intricate calendrical calculations.

Mystery cults

This is a general name for those esoteric forms of religious practice during Greco-Roman times that involved highly secret ceremonies to which only initiates were admitted (which is why some of them remain mysteries today). They include the Eleusinian mysteries (dedicated to Demeter and Persephone), Orphism (based on the poetry credited to Orpheus), Mithraism (involving the sacrifice of a bull to Mithras, originally a Persian deity) and various rites consecrated to Dionysus. Most incorporated some form of mystical "journey" to the underworld and back, featuring either total immersion in water or a rite within a dark and cavernous space; re-emergence had connotations of ritual cleansing or the start of a new life. Some additionally held out the promise of a blissful afterlife. Many of the cults were specific to one location or region.

Native North American religions

Fairly constant among hundreds of overlapping traditions are: reverence for a Great Spirit, who may reside in the heavens or be present in everything; thunderbirds – giant birds whose eyes flash lightning and whose wingbeats produce thunder and rain, and yet who are generally benevolent; an underworld that is basically malevolent but from which the herbs and grasses grow; the essential spirits of animals, birds and major plants who may correspond to tribal or personal totems; and the ancestral spirits of the tribe. Religious ritual is mostly communal (involving dancing and chanting), but for certain ceremonies or divinations may feature a shaman or wise woman.

Neolithic beliefs

Neolithic cultures (c.8000–3000 BCE) saw the rise of agriculture and settled communities. At the beginning of this time, society was probably matriarchal and the chief deities were accordingly female – the mother goddess, the Sun goddess and the fire goddess – with particular reference to the seasonal fertility of nature and the regular cycles of the female human body. Once armed defence of the settled community became necessary, a change of polarity in the dominant sex both of communal leaders and of deities became observable in most societies, although the importance of the mother goddess and the association with fertility were never forgotten.

Norse beliefs

Robust characters for hearty story-telling rather than religious entities, the Norse pantheon of the Vikings (9th–10th centuries) represented deifications of natural forces, of legendary founders of human skills and arts, and of the supposed inaugurators of festivals. But the final warlike gods who dwelt in Asgard, known as the Aesir (headed by Odin), were preceded by the more peaceable Vanir (probably headed by the mother goddess Freya) who included some even earlier folk-heroes, such as Thor. Elements of magic permeated throughout, reflected in the few ritual observances. The Vikings believed in an afterlife, known as Valhalla ("Hall of the Slain"). Kings and outstanding warriors were conducted there by the Valkyries (war goddesses) after death. They also conceived an apocalyptic vision of the world's final cataclysm – Ragnarok.

Polynesian beliefs

Much of Polynesian mythology (which includes the legends of New Zealand and Hawaii) is concerned with an account of the creation effected by the Sky and the Earth, which between them produced the gods, who in turn created the first woman and the first man. Such creative power is known as *mana*, a term that is also applied to the social power and influence that equates to rank in human society – a concept that is still of importance, as those of high rank are expected to remain ritually pure and to avoid all that is *tapu* (taboo).

Shamanism

Shamanism is a form of religious ritual – engaged in especially by those of animist or totemic beliefs – in which a (male or female) shaman enters a trance and so travels within the spirit world. The object may be to supplicate for a desired worldly benefit (such as a child, a cure, a good harvest, or rain), to placate or pacify a spirit identified as angry or malign, or to discover who is at fault for a crime or injury, particularly a sudden death. Europe and Antarctica are the only two continents in which shamans do not practise regularly.

Shinto

Shinto – the "way of the gods" (*kami*) – is the ancient indigenous religion of Japan and its tenets permeate the whole of Japanese custom and society. It centres on the belief that the *kami*, who are essentially spirits as much as gods, occupy and control all aspects and workings of nature in the world, some of them restricted to specific locations. Worshippers at the many shrines all over Japan clap their hands once or twice to attract the attention of the *kami* present, before making their supplication or ritual offering. Some Shinto rituals may be practised in the home; others constitute national festivals. Since the 19th century a number of different Shinto sects have emerged, some of which now have their own large, organized communities.

Sikhism

Founded in India by Guru Nanak in the 15th century, Sikhism centres on a belief in one transcendent God who permeates the world that he has created. Through successive incarnations – during which the guiding concepts must be work, worship and charity – a human soul may progress to final liberation and become truly God-centred (*gurmukh*) through the grace of God, who is regarded as the ultimate Guru (teacher). A community religion, Sikhism requires formal initiation into the faith and daily ritual worship and observances, although there is no priesthood as such and there are no regularly recurring holy days.

Sufism

Sufism is a highly ascetic Islamic mystical movement popularized first in the 12th century. Organized in the equivalent of monastic orders, each order (*tariqa*) has its own form of ecstatic worship (*dhikr*) that generally depends on repetition of either a word or phrase (such as the name of Allah) or of an activity that has the same connotations (such as the whirling of the Mevlevi dervishes). In modern times some orders have allowed degrees of congregational participation.

Sumerian religion

As befits the faith of a very early civilization (*c*.3000–2550 BCE), most of the religious beliefs of the Sumerians were directed toward general security and daily wellbeing – the main deities were those of the natural (elemental) forces, of agricultural and domestic fertility, and of victory in war. Great temples and towers were built to house the worshippers and their rites, although the tutelary deities might differ in each city-state. That worshippers believed that even their greatest kings were subject to divine will is evident from the figure of the legendary hero Gilgamesh, whose attempts to find immortality are frustrated by the gods.

Tantrism

Tantra, or Tantrism, is the use of certain esoteric practices – forms of meditation including yoga – to achieve a state of spiritual and physical ecstasy. Applied in some denominations of Hinduism and Buddhism, Tantrism particularly features *yantras* (mystical diagrams) and *mantras* (mystical repetitions or formulae). Hindu Tantra may involve sexual intercourse as a means of attaining enlightenment. Buddhist Tantrism usually stipulates the presence of a *guru* as instructor.

Vedic religion

The Aryans who invaded India during the 2nd millennium BCE carried with them the *Vedas*, their sacred texts – a vast compilation, in Sanskrit, of philosophy and liturgy, most of it in verse. A large proportion deals with several creation myths, featuring some of the gods that remain important in modern Hinduism – such as Vishnu and Prajapati (Brahma) – and others that have now faded into relative obscurity – such as Indra, Agni and Varuna. The stories have much to do with the physical and military difficulties of the Aryan invasion, but the *Vedas* remain sacred to Hindus today as the historical basis of their beliefs.

Voodoo

Basically a form of shamanism, Voodoo combines African and Christian religious elements and animism – its gods include deities from West Africa, Christian saints, and the spirits of natural forces and ancestors. Voodoo is prevalent in Haiti, although similar practices occur in the West Indies and some parts of northern South America. At almost all Voodoo ceremonies – after prior permission is obtained from the "gateway god" Legba (identified with St Peter) – the shaman and one or more of the worshippers enter a trance and are possessed (or "ridden") by one of the gods, so taking on the characteristics of the deity.

Zen Buddhism

Zen is a monastic tradition of Buddhism which entered Japan from China in the 12th century. It stresses the personal experience of enlightenment through meditation and a simple life lived close to nature. There are two main strands of Zen in Japan: Rinzai Zen, which seeks sudden and spontaneous enlightenment (often through the medium of a *koan*, or impossible conundrum, posed by a teacher); and Soto Zen, in which the achieving of enlightenment is a more gradual process through *zazen*, or "sitting meditation".

Zoroastrianism

In Persia (now Iran) *c*.1000 BCE, the religious philosopher Zoroaster (Zarathustra) created a new system of faith from the religious elements of his time. One of the earliest instances of monotheism, the new religion was dualist in nature, pitting the great creator god, Ahura Mazda, against the evil Hostile Spirit, Angra Mainyu, who in the fullness of time was finally to be vanquished. Zoroastrianism still has a number of followers. It is a community religion in which the priesthood is hereditary; communal daily prayers are required; other rites take place in the home or may be solemnized in a temple, which gives a sacred fire pride of place.

GLOSSARY

Cross references between glossary entries are in SMALL CAPITALS.

anima mundi Concept of "world soul" developed by the Greek philosopher Plato in the *Timaeus*.

atman Hindu name for the soul of each individual human being.

ba Believed by the ancient Egyptians to be the spiritual part of an individual. The *ba* of a dead person moved through the underworld and could revisit the Earth.

bodhisattva A Buddhist saint ("One whose Being is Enlightenment") who defers his own NIRVANA to help bring others to enlightenment.

brahman Hindu concept of absolute reality, the "universal soul"; a pure, impersonal consciousness whose authority is present in all things.

chakra According to yogic philosophy, a focal energy centre, or "wheel", within the body.

dharma In Hinduism, the principle of order governing the universe and individual lives; in Buddhism, the Truth as taught by the Buddha.

duhkha Buddhist word for suffering, also connoting imperfection and lack of satisfaction; the opposite of enlightenment.

geomancy Science aiming to set dwellings and activities in harmony with the physical and spiritual world, based on a belief that paths of energy run through the landscape.

hajj The Muslim pilgrimage to Mecca; the last of the Five Pillars of Islam.

ihram The state of purity for a Muslim pilgrim at Mecca.

ka In ancient Egypt, the life-force in gods and humans. Seen as an almost independent entity, the *ka* was thought to live on in the tomb after death, requiring food and drink to sustain it.

Kabbalah Jewish mystical tradition, originally orally transmitted, and having two aspects: practical, centring on prayer and meditation; and mystical, centring on the interpretation of mysteries in the Jewish Scriptures.

kami In Shinto beliefs a spirit or god, present in most aspects of nature and human life.

karma A similar, though not identical, concept in Hinduism, Jainism and Buddhism: essentially the law that each action in an individual life has consequences for the soul's next reincarnation.

mandala Magical diagram or map charting the journey through meditation to enlightenment, often used as a meditational aid.

mantra Sacred chant or ritual incantation, often used as an aid to meditation.

moksha In Hinduism and Jainism, the state of spiritual perfection enabling the soul to escape from all worldly ties and SAMSARA, the endless cycle of rebirth.

mudra Hindu and Buddhist symbolic hand gesture(s) used in rituals and dances.

nirvana Spiritual liberation ensuing from eradication of the greed, hatred and delusion that ties human beings to SAMSARA.

oni A Shinto demon, not always entirely evil.

salat Muslim ritual of movements and words to be performed five times a day; one of the Five Pillars of Islam.

samsara In Hinduism, Jainism and Buddhism, the concept of repeated reincarnation of the individual soul in the material world.

shakti Divine female creative energy.

stupa Cairn or mound used to house the ashes of Buddhist monks and holy relics.

tirtha In Hinduism and Jainism, a "ford" between earthly and divine realms where one pure in spirit may cross.

wakan To Native Americans, a spiritual essence which may reside in a wide range of natural or man-made objects.

wu wei Daoist principle of non-doing or non-action, not intent on any desired result.

yang In Chinese thought, the principle of masculinity, heat, light, heaven, creation and dominance; the opposite to YIN.

yin In Chinese thought, the principle of femininity, cold, dark, Earth and passivity; the opposite to YANG.

yoga A classical Indian philosophy teaching a practical means to enlightenment; uses a range of physical and contemplative techniques designed to free the higher, conscious element in humans from the inferior material world.

INDEX

Page numbers in *italics* refer to captions.

A

Aboriginal beliefs 18, 80, 92–3, *105*
Abraham (Ibrahim) 62, 131, 150
African beliefs 14, 56, 112, 116
afterlife 108–9, *see also* heaven; hell; paradise
Agni (god of fire) *97*
agriculture: and deities 16, 32, 52, 66, 82; crops as deities 87; harvest 22, 86, *see also* fertility
air 94–5, *see also* elements
Akedah (binding of Isaac) 62
Akkadian beliefs 82, 114
al-isra' (Night Journey of Muhammad) 110, 125, *160*
alchemy 50–1, *73*
altered states of consciousness 147
Amaterasu (Japanese Sun goddess) 32, *38*
Amazonia, shamans 82, *137*
Amitabha (Buddha) 143, 154
Anatolian beliefs 82, 86
ancestors: animals as men's ancestors 91
ancient Egypt: death 69, 71; dreams, interpretation 114; goddesses *42*, 51, 52, 86, *94*; gods *20*, 21, *41*, 50, 52; myths 21, 52; sacred animals *102*; spirit *76*; temples *36*
ancient Greece: dreams 114; goddesses 16, *16*, *42*, *43*, 51, 86, 91, 142; gods 31, 51, 64, 82, 114; heaven 124; myths 15, 16, 17, 108, 120; prayer 142; sacred prostitutes 52; spirit helpers 110–11; and the world soul 14–15, *see also* Demeter; Hades
ancient Rome: deities 31, 32–3, 85, *30*
angels 110, 122–3
anima mundi (world soul) 15
animals: gods as 91; masks in sacred ceremonies 14; men's ancestors 91; and reincarnation 117; sacred *99*, 102–6, *102*, *105*, 118; souls of 82; spirits of hunted animals 90
Apep (evil serpent of Egyptian myth) 21
Aphrodite (Greek goddess) *43*
Apocalypse 109; Angel of the Apocalypse *123*
Apocrypha *114*
archetypes (Jung) 115

architecture, sacred 36–37
arhats (Buddhism) 149, 156
Aristotle 26
Arjuna (Pandava warrior) 60
Ark of the Covenant (Judaism) 36
Ars Moriendi 69
Artemis (Greek goddess) 91
Arthur, King 136
aryasatya (Four Noble Truths) 29, 149, 156
ascents into the sky 18–19, *see also* heaven
asceticism 47, 138, *143*
Asklepios (Greek God of Medicine) 64, 114
astrology 25, 39, *see also* zodiac
astronomy, and religious festivals 24
atman (Hinduism) 20, 70, 71, 132, 138
atonement 134–5
Attis (Anatolian god) 82
Avalon (Celtic heaven) 124
avatars (Hinduism) 31, *100*
axis, world/cosmic/sacred 18–19
Ayers Rock (Uluru) *92*
Aztecs: deities *86*, *127*; sacrifice *62*; and the Sun 24–5, 50

B

ba (Egyptian mythology) 71
Babylonians, astronomical observations 24
Bacchus (Dionysus) 22, *83*, 147, *147*
Balinese beliefs 33, 56, 113, 118
Bar Mitzvah and Bat Mitzvah 150
Belovody (Russian paradise) 154
Beltane (Celtic festival) 118
Bhagavad Gita (Hinduism) 60
bhakti-marga (Hinduism) 131, 149
Bible 162, *162*; air, symbolism (Genesis) 94; angels in 110; descriptions of heaven 109; dreams in 114–15; exorcism in synoptic Gospels 113; Psalms 156; Yahweh (Old Testament God) 116, *see also* Apocrypha; Song of Songs
bird: Garuda *105*, *115*; spirit *75*, 76, *76*, *77*, *104*
Black Elk (Sioux Indian) 137
Blake, William 47, 156
Bodh Gaya 152
Bodhi Tree 28–9, *28*, 152, 156

bodhisattva 133, 149, *149*, 154, 156
body: association with zodiac *14*; Christian view 46, 47; and soul 46–7; spiritual 48–9
bonfires, seasonal 22
The Book of Changes 34
Book of the Dead (Egyptian) 20, 69
Book of the Dead (Tibetan) 67, 69
Book of Hours *23*
Brahma (Hindu god) *15*, 21, 31, *115*, 154
brahman (Hinduism) 30, 132
Buddha 29, 54, *133*, 146–7, *153*; asceticism 138; birth *160*; footprint *70–1*; life history 28–9, 152; miracles *160*, *161*; as ninth avatar of Vishnu 31; *parinirvana* 70, 152; enlightenment 156
Buddhism 29, 132, 149, 156; and the ego 28; faith 131; hand gestures in 58; heaven 124, *124*; and Hinduism 31; paradise 154; prayer *117*, 143; rapture 146; reincarnation 70; sacred sites 54; sleep 115; suffering 132–3; Tantra 53; teaching 149; temples 37; time, cyclical view of 20; Wheel of Life 108–9, *109*, *see also* Mahayana (Pure Land) Buddhism; *mandala*; Tantra; Tibetan Buddhism; Zen Buddhism
burial rituals 66–7, 69, 71
Bushmen of the Kalahari 56

C

calendars, sacred 22–3, *see also* festivals
Canaanite beliefs 16
candles: in Buddhism 156, *157*, *see also* light; Menorah
cave paintings, spiritual significance 90
celibacy 47, *see also* sexuality
Celtic beliefs 30, 46, 118, 120; fertility rites 86; goddesses 17, 85; heaven 124; and the hunt 91, *91*; paradise 154; spiritual rebirth 46
Ceres (Roman goddess) 87
Cerne Abbas, male figure 87
Cernunnos (Celtic Master of Animals) *91*
chakras (energy "wheels") 48, *48*, 49
Charon (boatman in Greek mythology) 108
Chichén Itzá (Mayan city) 24
China: divination in 34; emperors' sacrifices to

Heaven 117; geomantic system 88–9; weather as omen 25, *see also* Confucianism; Daoism

Chinese medicine 48, *64*, 65

Christ *see* Jesus Christ

Christianity: angels 122–3; annunciation *110*; architecture 36; death 66–7, 69, 71; dreams 115; Easter *22*, 24; exorcism in 113; faith 130, 131; fire, image in 76; heaven, concept of 109; hell *126*; miracles *161*; monasteries 138; origins 46–7; paradise 154–5; pilgrimages 54; prayer 142, *143*; religious services 58, 59; retreat *144, 145*; rituals 151; sacred figures *158, 159*; sacrifice 62, *63*; and sexuality 53; suffering 133; teaching 148; and the body 46–7; *see also* Bible; Orthodox church; Roman Catholic Church

churches, Christian, 36

comets 38, *38*

Communion chalice *131*

confession 135

Confucianism 150, 152; and *Yi Jing* 34

constellations, religious importance 38

corn plant, sacred: Inca *82*; Navaho 19

cornucopia *72*

cosmic axis 18–19

cosmic man *14*, *49*

creation: cosmological myth 15; Dreamtime 92–3; Greek myth 15; male and female elements 50; sexual union as symbol 52

cremation, Hindu 70–1, 85

Crick Stone (Men-an-tol) 46

crops *see* agriculture; corn

Crucifixion of Christ *63*, *68*

Crusades 60

Cybele (Anatolian goddess) 82, 86

cycles, death and rebirth 67, 70, 86, 108–109, 131, 138; time 20–1, *see also* reincarnation

D

daemon (spirit) 111

dance: in healing 64; sacred 56–7; Shiva as Nartaraja, Lord of the Dance 21

Daoism: beliefs 138; *Dao* (Way) 27, *163*; *Dao De Jing* 27, 50; depiction of hell *127*; erotic techniques *52*; and illness 64; incense in 116; Inner Alchemy 49; philosophy 26–7; sacred figure *158*; underworld map *120*; and *Yi Jing* 34, *see also* China; Zhuang Zhou

David (Hebrew Bible) 56

Day of the Dead *20*

death: confronting 120, 68–9; and the devil *70*; fear of 66–7; freedom in, and *gnosis* 46; preparation for 121; and sleep 115; spirit of *111*; survival after 70–1

Delphi 16, 35; *omphalos* 16, 18

Demeter (Greek goddess) 17, *42*, 86, *87*, 142

demons: soul stealers 112–13, *see also* devils

dervishes 56–7

devadasis (dance) 56

devas (Buddhist gods) 109

Devi (Hindu goddess) 43, 66, *see also* Kali

devils 112–13; death and *70*, *see also* demons

dharma 132, 152, 154

dhyana 140

Diana (Roman goddess) *90*, 91

Dionysus (Bacchus) 22, *83*, 147, *147*

disease 64–5, 113, 117

Divali (Hindu festival) 23, *23*, 118

divination 34–5

Dome of the Rock (Jerusalem) 18

domes: Islam 36; Orthodox Christian 36

dowsing 89

dragon *104*

Dream Journey 93

dreams 114–15; dream yoga 115; and Jung 15, 26; Zhuang Zhou's butterfly dream 26–7, *27*, *see also* sleep

Dreamtime/Dreaming (Aboriginal belief) 92–3

drugs, hallucinogenic, in healing 64

drum, shamanic *117*

duhkha (Buddhism) 29, 132, 149, 156

Dumuzi 51, 52

Durga (Hindu goddess) 16, *43*

E

Earth 98–9; as goddess 17; lines of force 88–9; as living creature 14; as mother 16–17, 42; sacred 80–1; and spirituality 14; violation of 16, *see also* elements; world

Easter 22, 24

eclipses, significance 38

ecstasy 56, 146–7, *see also* tantra

ego: and *guru* 149; illusion of 28–9, 66, 156; and suffering 132

Eightfold Path 149

elements: 14; deities 31, 32; in Greek myth 15, *see also* weather; individual elements

Elijah, Prophet *25*

Elysium (Greek heaven) 124

energy: Chinese medicine *64*; lines 88–9; winds of (*prana*) 48, 95

Enkidu (and Gilgamesh) 114

enlightenment 156–7

Epona (Celtic goddess) 17

Ethiopian beliefs *127*

Eurydice 120

Evangelists *159*

evil, spirits 31, 112

exorcism 64, *112*, 113, 118

Ezra, visions of *114*

F

female body, landscape as 16

female and male symbolism 50–1, 72

feng shui (Chinese geomancy) 88–9

fertility 86–7; deities 32, 80, 82; egg, as symbol of rebirth 22; rituals *57*, *see also* agriculture

festivals 96, 118, 135; and astronomy 24; Hindu 22, 23, *23*, 24, 118; Japanese 33; Jewish 23, 62, 135; and lunar calendar 24; seasonal 22, 82, 118

figures, sacred 158–9

fire 96–7; festivals 22; as image for soul 76, *see also* cremation; elements; light

flood of Babylon *100*

forgiveness 134–5

Four Noble Truths (Buddhism) 29, 149, 156

Freud, Sigmund 114

funerals: Hindu 70–1; Japanese 32

G

Gabriel (Jibreel, angel) 110, *125*, 136, 152–3

Gaia (Greek Earth goddess) 16, *16*, 86

Ganges Basin, as sacred site 54, *84*, 85
Garden of Eden 154–5, *155*
Gardens of Paradise (Islam) 154
Garuda (celestial bird in Hinduism) *105*, *115*
Geb (Egyptian god) 52
gender 50–51, *51*, 72–73, *see also* sexuality
geomancy 88–9
ghosts: ancestors 112; Buddhist 108; Hindu 70;
    Japanese *109*; as uncontrollable forces 112
Gilgamesh 114, 120
Gnosticism 46–7
goddesses 42–3; Earth 16; of spring *22*; sexual
    union with gods 51, 72
gods 32–3, 40–1; human characteristics31;
    divine intervention 116–17; divine revelation
    114–15; impersonation 117; pantheons
    30–1; Roman *30*; and goddesses 51, 72
gold *99*
Green Man (spirit) 82, 86, *86*
Grim Reaper 66, *66*
guardian spirits 111
guru 149
Guru Nanak 150, *158*

H

Hades (Greek god of the underworld) 17, 108,
    120, 126
hajj (Islam pilgrimage to Mecca) 54–5, *55*
Hallowe'en 118, *118*
hallucinogenic drugs, in healing 64
halo, as energetic aura 49
hand gestures (*mudras*) 58, *59*
Hanukkah (Jewish festival) 23
harpy *76*
harvest *22*, 86
Hasidic Jews, dance 57
Hawaiian mythology 51
healing 64–5; ceremonies 117
heaven 124–5; celestial realms 38–9; Christian
    109, *see also* afterlife; paradise
heavenly bodies, significance 38–9
Heisenberg, Werner 35
hell 66–7, 108, 126–7, *see also* afterlife;
    underworld
Hera (Greek goddess) 51, *142*

herbal medicines *65*; to stimulate dreams 114
Herero people, beliefs 85
hermaphrodite *73*
hermits 144
heroes 120; archetype of hero 61
Hesse, Herman 55
hieros gamos (sacred marriage) 51
Hinduism 53, 112, 117, 132, 148–9; *atman* 20,
    70, 71, 132, 138; avatars 31, *100*; and
    Buddhism 31; death and the soul 70–1, 85;
    divine intervention 117; and ego 28; faith
    131; festivals 22, 23, *23*, 24, 118; goddesses
    16–17, *42*, 43, 51, 66, 67, *115*, 118, 140;
    gods 15, 21, 31, *41*, 115, 116, 154; hand
    gestures in 58; heaven 124; Kundalini Yoga
    49; Mount Meru 19; pantheon 30–1;
    paradise 154; prayer 58; reincarnation 70;
    sacred sites 54, 85, 108; suffering 132;
    temples 37, 54; texts 60; time 20–1;
    wandering holy men and women 138, *see
    also* Indian beliefs; Krishna; *mandala*;
    moksha; *shakti*; Shiva; Tantra; Vishnu
Hippocrates 64
Holi (Hindu festival) 22, 24
holy fool 143
Holy Grail 136, *136*
Homer 114
Horned Serpent (Native American divinity) 80
Horus (Egyptian god) *41*
hotspots (Aboriginal sacred places) 93
household gods 32–3
Huichol shamans 111, *137*
Huitzilopochtli (Aztec Sun god) 50, *62*
hunting 90–1; Inuit spirits 117
Hygeia 64

I

Ibrahim (Abraham) 62, 131, 150
icons, Orthodox Church 69, *142*
'Id al-Adha 150
'Id al-Fitr 150
ihram (Islam ritual purity) 54
Iliad, the 114
illness 64–5, 113, 117
illusion: of ego 28–9; and the world 26–7

immortality 74
Inanna 51, 52, 86
Incas, sacrifice 63
incense, significance 116
incubus 112–13
India, miracles 160; temple prostitutes 56
Indian beliefs: astrological chart *39*; mother
    goddesses 16, *see also* Hinduism
initiation rites: Aboriginal 93; Christ's 136
Inuit beliefs 90–1, 102, 111, 116–17
Ireland: fertility rituals 86, passage-grave 24, *see
    also* Celtic beliefs
Isaac 62
Ise complex, Japan 32
Ishtar (Akkadian goddess) 82
Isis (Egyptian goddess) 51, 86, *94*
Islam: angels 122; faith 130, 131; *hajj* 54–5, *55*;
    heaven *125*; Holy Days 150; *jihad* 60, 131;
    miracles *160*; paradise 154; prayer 59, *59*,
    143, *143*; Ramadan 24, 150; repentence
    134; representation of deity 36–7; rituals
    150; sexuality 53; suffering 133; teaching
    148; *see also* Koran; Mecca; mosques
Izanagi (Japanese god) 32, 52, 120
Izanami (Japanese goddess) 32, 52, 120

J

Jacob (Hebrew Bible) 114–15
jade *99*
Jainism *139*; and the ego 28; Mount Meru 19;
    sacred sites 54; time, cyclical view of 20, 21,
    see also Mahavira (Jain saint)
Jalal al-Din al-Rumi 56
Japan: festivals 33; ghosts *109*; religion 32;
    warriorship 60–1, *see also* Shinto
Jerusalem: 31, 54; and Judaism 23, 36, *see also*
    Dome of the Rock; Temple of Solomon
Jesse tree *19*
Jesus Christ 153; baptism *101*; Crucifixion *63*,
    68; descent into Hell *126*; divine lover of
    soul 51; healing powers 64; in Holy Grail
    136; Pantocrator 36; Passion 69, 133;
    sacrifice 116; scourging *132*; teacher 148
jihad (Islam) 60, 131
jnana-marga (Hinduism) 149

Jonah and the Whale *130*
Joseph (Hebrew Bible) 114–15
journeys, of heroes 120–1
Judaism: air, symbolism 94; angels 122; dance
    57; faith 130, 148; festivals 23, 62, 135;
    heaven 124; Kabbalah 49; mourning 69;
    paradise 154–5; penitence 134–5; services
    59; representation of deity and 36; rituals
    150; sexuality 53; suffering 133;
    synagogues, representation in 36; teaching
    148; world axis 18; "World to Come" 109
judgment after death 66–7
Jung, Carl 15, 26, 47, 66, 115
jyotis (Vedic "heavenly bodies") *39*

K

ka (Egyptian mythology) 71
Ka'bah (Mecca) 18, 54–5
Kabbalah (Jewish mystical system) 49
Kali (Hindu goddess) 16, 66, *67*, *140*, *see also*
    Devi
kami (Japanese gods) 32, 33, 81, 84, 112
karma 70, 124, 132
Kedarnath, Hindu temple *54*
Kierkegaard, Søren 130
Knights of the Round Table 136
Konarak, Temple of the Sun 39, 50
Koran 36–7, 110, 115, 136, 143, 148, 153, 162,
    162; Muhammad's Night Journey *125*
Krishna (Hindu god) 31, *41*, 60, *72*, 116, 117
Kunia (Sky Heroes) 92
Kyudo 61

L

Lakota tribe 81
Lakshmi (Vishnu's consort) *115*, 118
Lands of the Blessed 124
landscape 89, 16, 80, 84
Lares (Roman household gods) 33
last judgment 66–7
ley lines 89
leyaks (Balinese spirits) 113
Li Ji 150
light: candles *97*, 156, *157*; and festivals 23, 96,

118, *see also* fire
Lilith *47*
lines of force 88–9
linga (phallus) 52–3
lotus flower *100*
love mystics 51
lunar calendar, and holy festivals 24

M

madness, treatment of sufferers 64
Magna Mater (Roman goddess) 86
Mahabharata (Hindu sacred text) 116
Maharishi Mahesh Yogi 147
Mahavira (Jain saint) 54, 138, *see also* Jainism
Mahayana (Pure Land) Buddhism 133, 143,
    149, 154
Mahisha (Hindu demon) *43*
maize, sacred 19, *82*
male and female symbolism 50–1, 72–73
mandala 19, 37, 68, 140
Manichaeism 46, 47
mantras 142
Maori beliefs 80
maps: of spiritual path 146, *see also mandala*
Mara (Buddhist demon) 156
marriage: gods and goddesses 51, 72, 86; of
    heaven and earth 51; Shinto weddings 32
The Marriage of Heaven and Hell (Blake) 47
Mary Magdalene *135*
masks: animal 14; dance *56*; of gods 117
Master of Animals 90
matsuri (Japanese festivals) 33
May Queen 86
Mayan mythology 18, 24, 87
maypole dances 57
Mecca 18; pilgrimage to 54–5
medicine 64–65
meditation 48, 66, 140–1
memento mori 66
Menorah (Judaism) 23, *96*, 156
Milarepa (Tibetan mystic) 68, 145, *145*
Minerva (Roman goddess) 85
miracles 160–1
Mithras (Persian god) *105*
mitzvah (Judaism) 150

moksha (Hinduism) 20, 28, 131, 148
monasteries 138, 144–5
Mongols *52*
monks 144–5
monotheistic beliefs 30, 31, 40, 53, 130, *see also*
    Christianity; Islam; Judaism
Moon: as female symbol 50; hare in the Moon
    74; importance 24, 25, 38; lunar calendar 24
morris dances 57
mosques: 36; Samarra *150*, *see also* Islam
mother: earth as 16–17, *17*, 80–1; goddesses 86
Mount Athos *144*
Mount Fuji 81, *81*
Mount Meru 19, 37, 139
Mount Sinai *80*
mourning, rituals 69
mudras (hand gestures) 58, *59*
Muhammad 152, *153*; ascent to heaven *125*;
    encounters with angels 110, 136; visions 115
mummification 71
mystics *see* love mystics; Sufis

N

nadi 48
Nataraja *see* Shiva
Native Americans: 14, 16, 57, 80, 81;
    Cheyenne 81; Cree Moon image *24*; prayer
    58; vision quests 137; Navaho 19, 117;
    Ojibway 34; Plains Indians 111 Sioux 14,
    81, 137
nature, worship of 14, 32, 82–3, 117
Nazca plain, markings 88, *88*
near-death experiences 108
Neolithic beliefs 16, 24
New Year festivals 118, 135
Newgrange (Irish passage-grave) 24
Nike (goddess) 122, 142
nimbus, as energetic aura 49
nirvana 149, 156
Norse myth: Odin 40, 62; ship burning *96*;
    Yggdrasil *19*
Nuliajak (Inuit sea spirit) 116–17
Numbakula (Aboriginal divine being)
    18
Nut (Egyptian goddess) 52

O

Odin (Norse god) *40*, 62
Odysseus 120
offerings, in prayer ritual 58
Old Woman of the Seals 90–1
omphalos 16, 18
oni (Japanese demons) 112
oracles, divination 34–5
orgy, ritual 86–7
Orpheus myth 120
Orthodox Church: and death 69; domes 36; icons 69, *142*; monasteries *144*; prayer 143
Osiris 22, 51

P

pagan origin of festivals *22*
Paleolithic cave paintings 90
Pan (Greek god) 82
Panacea 64
pantheistic beliefs 30
Papua New Guinea, beliefs 80
paradise 154–5, *see also* afterlife; heaven
parinirvana (Buddha) 70, 152
Parvati (Hindu goddess) 16–17, 51
Paschal Candle *97*
Passion (Christ) 69, 133
Passover (Judaism) 24, 150, *151*
Patanjali (Hindu philosopher) 140
penitence 134–5
Persephone (Greek myth) 17
Perusa (Hinduism) 53
petroglyphs *99*
philosophy: and ego 28–9; illusion and reality 26–7; philosopher's stone 51, *see also* Plato
phoenix *74*
pilgrimage 54–5
pitrpaksha (Hinduism) 112
planets: religious importance 38, *see also* zodiac
plants: holy 19, *82*, 117; as spirit teachers 111
Plato 15, 26, 46, 50, 68, 110–11
Polynesian beliefs 14, 51
possession, diabolic 64, 113
prana 48, *95*
prasena (Tibetan method of divination) 35

prayer 116, 58–9, 142–3; "breastplate" 142; fertility prayers 87; healing 64; "Ionica" 142; Jesus prayer 143; Muslim 59; prayer wheel, Buddhism *117*
preta (ghosts) 70
prostitutes, sacred 52, 56
Psalms 156
Psychology and Alchemy, Carl Jung 15
Pythagoras (Greek mathematician) 26

Q

Qiniandian (Chinese religion) 117
Qur'an *see* Koran

R

Ra (Egyptian Sun god) *20*, *21*, 50
rabbis (Judaism) 148
Rahit (Sikh code of discipline) 60
rain deities 86, *86*, 87
rainbow *138*
Rainbow Serpent (Sky Hero) 92, 93
Raja Yoga *47*, 140
Rama (Hindu god) 31, 116
Ramadan (Islam) 24, 150
Ramayana (Hindu sacred text) 116
reincarnation and rebirth 67, 70, 74, 86, *see also* cycles, of death and rebirth
retreat 144–5
revelation 31, 114–15, 156
rituals 150–1
rivers, spiritual significance 84–5, 108
Roman Catholic Church: penance 135; prayer 58, 143
rosaries 143
Rosh Ha-Shanah (Jewish festival) 62, 135
ruku (Islamic bow) 59

S

Sabbath (Jewish) 150
sacred sites 36–7, 54, 84, 92
sacrifice 62–3; fertility 87; in prayer ritual 58; Vedic horse sacrifice 86
Saints: Augustine 47, *71;* Bernard of Clairvaux

51; Catherine *158*; Francis 116; Isaac of Syria 144; John of the Cross 138, 146; Michael 89, *89*; Patrick 142; Paul, 69; Stephen *71*; Teresa of Avila 51, 146
Samhain (Celtic festival) 118
samsara 20, 28, 109, 156
Samurai (Japan) *61*
Sangha (Buddhist monks) 152
sati (self-immolating widow) *130*
scapegoat 118
scarab beetle *74*
science: and divination 35; medicine as 64
seasons: deities 31, 82; festivals 22, 82, 118
Seder (Judaism) 150, *151*
Sedra (Inuit sea spirit) 116–17
Senoi beliefs 114
Seraphim *123*
Serpent Mound *81*
sexuality: and Christianity 47, 53; goddesses 42; sexual energy and spiritual life 52–3; sexual partner, search for 50; sexual intercourse, 72, *see also* gender
Shaker Church 57
"Shaking Tent" (Ojibway divination lodge) 34
shakti (Hinduism) 53, 85, 140, *141*
shamanism 18–19, 90–1, 108, 110, 111; divination 34; drum *117*; healing 74; incarnation of souls 82; initiation 121; Nepalese 85; "soul flight" 110; spirit power 116–17; trances 147; vision quests 137, *137*
Shangri-La 124
Shinto 33, 58, 81, 84, 112; gods and goddesses 32, *38*, 52, 120; spirits *83*
Shiva (Hindu god) 31, 51, *53*, 67, *115*, *141*, 154; dancing *21*; linga 52, 53; as Nataraja 21
shofar *135*
shrines: Hinduism 117; Shinto 32
Shri Yantra 68–9
Sikhism 60, 143, 150; sacred figure *158*
silver *99*
simarani (Sikh rosary) 143
Siren *76*
sky: symbolism 18–19; sacred 24–5
Sky Heroes (Aboriginal belief) 92
Sky Pole (Aboriginal belief) 18
sleep: in Buddhism and Hinduism 115; and

death 115; soul's vulnerability in 112–13, *see also* dreams

"smudging" (North American prayer ritual) 58

Socrates 26

solstice, festivals 22, 24

Soma 74

Song of Songs 51

soul: Ancient Greek theories 26; animal souls 82; and the body 46–7; loss of, as diagnosis 64; natural phenomena as possessing 14; survival 70–1, *see also* spirit

speaking in tongues 146

spirit: forms of 76, *see also* soul

springs (water), spiritual significance 85

stairway to heaven *125*

standing stones *98*

stars: religious importance 38, *see also* constellations; sky; zodiac

stigmata *116, 123*

stupa (Buddhist temple) 37

Styx (river) 108

Sufis: meditation 140; retreat 144–5; dance 56

Sulis (Celtic goddess) 85

Sumerian beliefs 86, *see also* Inanna

sun: Aztec mythology 24–5, 50; Chariot of the Sun *39*; gods and goddesses *20*, 21, 32, *38*, *39*, 50, *62*, 63; male symbol 50; religious importance 21, 24, 38; solstice *22*, 24

Sun Dance (Native American) 57, *133*

supplication, prayers of 58

Surya (Vedic Sun god) 39, 50

Symposium (Plato) 50, 110–11

synagogues 36

synchronicity, and divination 34

T

Talmud (Jewish sacred writings) 109, 133

Tammuz *22*, 82

Tantra: and death 66, 68–9; ritual sexual congress 53; Tantric discipline 48

Tao *see* Dao

Tarot cards *35*

templum (origin of "temple") 36

temples: Buddhist 37; Temple of Heaven, (China) 117, 150; Hindu 37; nature of 36; of

Solomon 18, *125*; Shinto 32

thanksgiving 58, 150

Theravada school of Buddhism 149

thunder, as omen 25

Thunderbird Drum *94–5*

Tibetan Buddhism: death 67, 68, 69; holy fool 143; *mandala* 19; oracles 35; prayer flag *94*; retreat 145; Vajrayana Buddhism 25, *see also* Buddhism

Timaeus (Plato) 15

time, cycles of 20–1

Tir-na-n'Og (Celtic paradise) 154

tirthas (Hinduism) 108

Torah (Judaism) 36, 130, 148, 150, 156, *163*

torii (Shinto shrines) 32; gateway *33*

torture, in Hell 67

totem poles *22*

trance, induced by dance 56

transcendent states 146, 147

transubstantiation *131*

trees: Banyan Tree 85; Ceiba tree (Mayan mythology) 18; Dodona Tree *95*; of Enlightenment 156; in Jainism 21; of Knowledge *63*, 155; Tree of Life 85, *101*; Sioux legend 137; *see also* Bodhi Tree; World Tree

troglodytes (monks) 145

U

Uluru (Ayers Rock) *92*

unconscious: and dreams 115; and the soul 15

underworld 120–1; Daoist map *120*; Earth goddesses and 17; heroes visiting 120; Ra in *20*; soul's descent *120*, *see also* hell

unicorn *73*

V

Vajrayana Buddhism 25

vampires 113

Vedic beliefs 39, 50, 52, 86

"Venus" figures 86

Virgin Mary *43*

Vishnu (Hindu god) 21, 31, *115*, 116, 117, 154

vision quests 136–7

visions 114–15, 156; ecstatic 146–7

voodoo *113*

Voyage of Bran 120

warrior cultures 60–1

water 84–85, 100–1, 108; ablution 58; paradise 154; underworld 121; 84–5, *see also* elements

weather 25, 116–17, *see also* elements

Wheel of Life (Buddhism) 108–9, *109*

Wheel of Time (Hinduism) 20, 154

whirling dervishes 56–7

"witch doctors" 64

women, and sexuality in Christianity 53

Word of God 131, 148, 162

world: human, and gods 32–3; and illusion 26–7, *see also* Earth

world axis 18–19, *see also* Mount Meru

world soul 14–15

World Tree 18–19, *19*, 62, 108

wu wei (Daoist concept of non-being) 27

Y

Yahweh (God) 116

Yama (Lord of Death) 67, 118

Yamantaka (Tibetan conqueror of death) *67*

yantra 140, *140*

Yei (Navajo gods) 117

Yggdrasil (Norse myth) *19*

Yi Jing (The Book of Changes) 34

yin and yang 50, *64*

yoga *47*, 48, 49, 115, 140

Yom Kippur 135

yoni (vulva) 52–3

yugas (Hinduism) 21, 154

Z

Zen Buddhism 131, 138, *162*

Zeus (Greek god) 51

Zhuang Zhou 26–7, 68, *see also* Daoism

zodiac 38–9; animal gods 102; and parts of the body 14; origin 24, *see also* astrology

ACKNOWLEDGMENTS

The publishers wish to thank the following photographers and organizations for their kind permission to reproduce the copyright material in this book.

KEY:

AA&A: Ancient Art and Architecture
AKG: Archiv für Kunst und Geschichte, London
BAL: Bridgeman Art Library
BL: British Library
BM: British Museum
TSI: Tony Stone Images
V&A: Victoria and Albert Museum, London
WFA: Werner Forman Archives

t: top, b: bottom, c: centre, l: left, r: right

6 Museum of Mankind, London; 7 BAL; 9 Christie's Images © ADAGP, Paris and DACS, London 1997; 10 BAL/BL; 11l V&A; 11r Hutchison Library; 15 BAL/V&A; 16 e.t. Archive; 17 Biblioteca Apostolica Vaticana; 18–19 e.t. Archive; 20t Musuem of Mankind, London; 20b Michael Holford; 22 Zefa; 23 e.t. Archive/V&A; 24 WFA/BM; 25 BAL; 27 DBP Archive; 29 BM; 30–31 e.t. Archive; 32 Elizabeth Whiting; 35 e.t. Archive; 36 Norma Joseph/Royal Geographical Society; 37 Pictorial Press of China/DBP Archive; 38 Michael Holford/V&A; 39 BAL/BM; 40-41 BAL/Bibliothèque Royale de Belgique; 41l Christie's Images; 41r DBP Archive; 42t Jurgen Liepe; 42bl BAL/Musée Guimet; 43tl DBP Archive; 43tr Michael Holford; 43b Hutchison Library; 46 Scala; 47 BAL; 48 AA&A; 49 Jean-Loup Charmet; 50 BM; 51 Tate Gallery, London © ADAGP, Paris and DACS, London 1997; 52r BAL; 53 BM; 54 Paul Harris/Royal Geographical Society; 55–56 BAL; 58–59 BAL/V&A; 61 Michael Holford; 62 e.t. Archive/Chavez Ballon Collection; 63l BAL; 63r BAL/Bibliothèque Nationale, Paris; 65

Superstock Fine Art; 67 AA&A; 68 BAL/Monasterio de El Escorial, Spain; 69 Graham Harrison; 70t Museum of Mankind, London; 70b Glen Allison/TSI; 71 BAL/San Tomé, Toledo, Spain; 72 BAL/BL; 73l Mary Evans Picture Library; 73r Michael Holford/BM; 74l, 74c, 74r Michael Holford; 76 Scala/Museo Gregorino Egizio, Vatican; 77l National Gallery, London; 77r BM; 80 BL; 81t BAL/Oriental Museum, University of Durham; 81b Ohio Historical Society, Ohio; 82 WFA; 83t Scala/Museo Nazionale Napoli; 83r J. Holmes/Panos Pictures; 84 BM; 85 Hutchison Library; 86 e.t. Archive/National Gallery of Mexico; 87 e.t. Archive/Palace Barborina, Rome; 88t Images Colour Library; 88b Mick Sharp Photography; 90 e.t. Archive/Museum of Archaeology, Naples; 92t Hutchison Library; 92b Images Colour Library; 93 Hutchison Library; 94t Paul Harris/ Royal Geographical Society; 94b AKG/Royal Library, Copenhagen; 95 John Bigelow Taylor; 96 BL; 97 BAL/Louvre; 98 Hutchison Library; 99l Corbis/Smithsonian Institution; 99r Images Colour Library; 100l Michael Holford; 100r e.t. Archive/El Escorial; 101 BL; 102 DBP Archive; 103 BL (Add. 11695 f240); 104tl BAL/Oriental Museum, University of Durham; 104tr Michael Holford/BM; 104b Museum of Fine Arts, Boston; 105 BAL; 105bl AA&A; 105br Robert Harding Picture Library; 108 DBP Archive; 109l C.M. Dixon; 109r BAL/V&A; 110 BAL/Museo Diocesana, Cortona, Italy; 110–111 BAL/Louvre, Paris; 111r BAL/Allbright Knox Gallery, Buffalo, New York; 112 e.t. Archive/National Gallery, London; 113l Superstock Fine Arts; 113r DBP Archive; 114 BL (Add. 47672 f170 detail); 115 WFA/National Gallery, Prague; 116 BAL; 117t, 117b DBP Archive; 119 BAL; 120 Julian Rothenstein; 121 Scala/Museo Paestum; 122l e.t. Archive; 122r e.t. Archive/Royal Fine Arts Museum, Anvers, Belgium; 123l e.t. Archive/

Anagni Cathedral, Italy; 123r Christie's Images; 124t DBP/Wat Buddhapadipa, London; 124b BAL; 125 BAL/BL; 126l BAL; 126r e.t. Archive; 127l Mary Evans Picture Library; 127r BL (Or641 f267r); 130l Hutchison Library; 130r BAL/Scrovegni Chapel, Padua; 132 e.t. Archive/Scrovegni Chapel, Padua; 133t America Hurrah, New York City; 133b Jean-Leo Dugast/Panos Pictures; 134 Bodleian Library, Oxford (Ms Ouseley Add. 17.b.f4v); 135 BAL/Palazzo Bianco, Genoa; 136 e.t. Archive; 137t DBP Archive; 137b DBP Archive; 139 BL (Add. Or1814); 140 BM; 141 BL; 142 AKG; 143t DBP Archive; 143b BAL/BL; 144 Piers Vitebsky; 145t WFA/Philip Goldman Coll.; 145b Hutchison Library; 147 BAL; 148t Jean-Loup Charmet; 148b BAL/Fitzwilliam Museum, Cambridge; 149 AA&A; 151 BAL; 152–3 BAL/BL; 153 e.t. Archive; 154 e.t. Archive; 155 BAL; 158l Ann & Bury Peerless; 158c Michael Holford/BM; 158r BAL; 159l AKG/Library of Trinity College, Dublin; 159r Michael Holford; 160l e.t. Archive; 160c AKG; 160–1 Scala; 161b Ann & Bury Peerless; 162bl e.t. Archive; 162–3t BL (Add. 54782 f131v); 162br WFA; 163t BL (Kings I f.F21); 163 e.t. Archive

COMMISSIONED ARTWORK CREDITS
Matthew Cooper: 2/3, 13, 45, 79, 107, 125l, 129, 157
Alison Barrett: 23b, 28/29, 33, 34/35, 39r, 52t, 54/55, 72r, 74bc, 77c, 95b, 97l, 98l, 99r, 100t, 103r, 131, 135b, 150, 161r
Louisa St Pierre: 1, 4, 14, 19r, 21, 24/25t, 27l, 38br, 40l, 42br, 47r, 57, 60, 66, 73t, 74t, 76r, 86t, 91, 96r, 97c, 101r, 102r, 105bl, 118, 124/125, 138, 146
Hannah Fermin: 51l

The publishers would also like to thank Liz Cowen, Susan Martineau and Mike Darton for their contributions to this book.